PRAISE FOR *FUTUREGOOD*

"*FutureGood* provides a road map for young leaders committed to making an impact! Trista Harris's expertise will change the way you think about the future." —Simone Gbolo, national director, Public Policy and International Affairs Program

"In a complex, volatile environment, leaders can't merely react to disruptive change: they need a model for shaping the future. *FutureGood* provides an easy-to-understand model that helps leaders move to action." —Luz María Frías, president and CEO, YWCA Minneapolis

"In the 21st century, leaders can't merely react to disruptive change: they need a model for shaping the future. *FutureGood* provides an easy-to-understand model that helps leaders move to action." —Y. Elaine Rasmussen, CEO, Social Impact Strategies Group

"The innovative and smart tools offered in *FutureGood* offer great insight and opportunities for us to make a better future today. It is a remarkable resource for all of us." —Kara Inae Carlisle, vice president of programs, McKnight Foundation

"This is a must-read guide for people that are working to solve society's greatest challenges." —Sherece West, president and CEO of Winthrop Rockefeller Foundation

"Anyone who has ever wanted to make the world a better place will absolutely love the simple and powerful tools in this book."
—Aaron Dorfman, president and CEO, National Committee for Responsive Philanthropy

"Many of us want to create a better future but are unsure of how to make this a reality. Reading the strategies in *FutureGood* will help you get there." —Adrienne Jordan, director of project and risk management, Minnesota Super Bowl Host Committee

"*FutureGood* reminds us that we can be founders of the future and offers key insights and tools to help bring about all the good that we can envision." —Diane Tran, system director of Neighborhood Integration, HealthEast

"The future promises an unknown landscape; in *FutureGood*, Trista Harris provides maps to show you what is coming next." —Lorrie Janatopoulos, former planning director, Arrowhead Economic Opportunity Agency

"Big business and government have used futurism for decades to help them understand where the world is headed and how to effectively get in front of it, shape it, or react to it. With Trista's book, those of us trying to make the world a better place have a key to unlock this powerful tool. Bravo!" —Athena Adkins, president, BetterWorld Partners

"With *FutureGood*, Trista Harris coalesces cutting-edge innovation techniques, empowering any of us who are on a mission to make the world a better place with breakthrough mindsets and practical tools." —Nicholas Haan, PhD, Singularity University; faculty chair, Global Grand Challenges

"Too many of us are pessimistic about the future. Reading the strategies in *FutureGood* will help you move to positive action." —Jim Rowader, vice president and general counsel, Employee and Labor Relations at Target

FUTURE GOOD

HOW TO USE FUTURISM TO SAVE THE WORLD

TRISTA HARRIS

ISBN: 978-1-63489-170-7

Printed in the United States of America
First Printing: 2018

23   22   21   20   19   7   6   5   4   3

Cover design by Zoe Norvell
Interior design by Kim Morehead

Wise Ink Creative Publishing
807 Broadway St. NE, Suite 46
Minneapolis, MN 55413
www.wiseink.com

To order, visit www.itascabooks.com or call 1-800-901-3480. Reseller discounts available.

To my husband, Mark, who has always made our future together something I look forward to.

To my children, Nia and Marcus, who are the two most important reasons I work to build a better future.

And to every single member of the FutureGood community: thank you for making our collective future brighter.

TABLE OF CONTENTS

INTRODUCTION

We're the generation that can't afford to wait.
The future started yesterday, and we're already late.

—John Legend

In 2008, I landed my dream job as executive director of the Headwaters Foundation for Justice. Headwaters was supporting ideas and leaders that came from marginalized communities and that had unique solutions to seemingly intractable problems of racism, economic injustice, environmental decline, and social change. I was a few months into my job when the stock market had the largest single-day dip since 1987's crash. That dip was followed by continuing drops and then a recession that, at its worst, decreased the value of our small foundation's assets by more than 30 percent. All of my painstaking research into how the foundation had operated in the past and a one-year-old strategic plan done by handsomely paid and highly trained experts suddenly became useless.

As it became clearer that this dip in the market was not going to be a short-term problem, I participated in many meetings with foundation and nonprofit leaders that basically said: "This is going to be a rough ride for nonprofits, and many of you are not going to make it through this recession. Start planning now how you will merge with a larger, stronger organization so that some of your programs to make the community better will make it through." At a time when the community needed so much more from foundations and nonprofits, we were forced to scale back and enter survival mode.

When I asked my foundation colleagues about adjusting our funding strategies to help nonprofits adjust to this new reality, there was a lot of talk about wanting to increase foundation payout. But the decreasing assets meant that fewer resources would be going out to the community. Foundations also adjusted their strategies to deal with more urgent community needs as the recession hit families hard. As a result, many foundations focused their grantmaking on "essential services" like food shelves and homeless shelters to help families that had been hit hardest by the recession and resulting job losses.

For Headwaters' grantees, which were leading community organizing efforts to deal with the root causes of economic justice issues, most funding completely dried up. It was a trying time, and I wondered if our organization and the dozens of nonprofits that we supported would survive. We started to accept that the economy would be terrible for a long time and to develop strategies rather than wait for things to get better.

Luckily, we were spurred on by two social justice thinkers and a new viewpoint from a long-standing organizing group. First, Beth Zemsky, an organizational development expert and community organizer, gave a training to our grantees about movement arcs. Society moves in arcs, and at the top of the arc, almost everybody believes in the same things (for example, that our home values will always increase). As that idea dies down, another idea rises (taking on debt from our homes is unsustainable, and we need to live a much simpler lifestyle). You can hold on to the old idea until it runs into the ground, or you can jump onto the next arc and be a forerunner.

Movement arcs look like this:

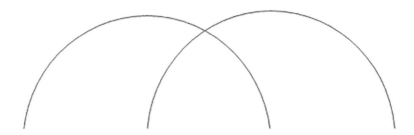

The second thinker was Suzanne Pharr, an organizer and political strategist, who met with a small group of our donors and grantees and said something that at first felt counterintuitive: that the economic crisis might be the best thing that has happened for organizers working on economic justice issues. When it felt like times were good, no one cared about the structural inequality in our economic system. But when the economy collapsed, the issue suddenly became much more real for many Americans. She suggested that our organizations would have new allies and our message would resonate with the masses who had been so personally impacted by the economic collapse.

The last influence was a youth-organizing training that I attended with the Children's Defense Fund. I participated in a few days of training about how to organize and influence critical community issues. Some of the participants were young people who had aged out of the foster-care system and were learning about organizing so they could reform the system. The trainer, Pakou Hang, told the group that during the next break they were going to practice the messaging and influencing skills they'd just learned by calling their elected officials about health-care reform. One of the young women raised her hand and said, "I just recently turned eighteen and have aged out of the foster-care system which raised me. I have really appreciated this training and have learned so many things that will help me change this broken system when I get home. During the break I will also make phone calls, but I will talk with my elected official about why the foster-care system needs to be reformed."

I got a little teary-eyed when I heard the young woman speak and felt so proud that, even at such a young age, she would use her experience to make the system better for the kids behind her.

But suddenly, I was pulled out of my feelings when I heard the trainer say, a little harshly, "No, you are not. You are going to make the call about health-care reform." I was shocked. Why would she tell this earnest young woman that she shouldn't advocate to fix the system that had had such a looming presence in her life? Pakou continued: "This is a time when health-care reform is possible if we all push together and hold our elected officials accountable. If we all leave and do our own thing, nothing will change because there won't be enough momentum. We have to work together to make this happen, and when it is time for foster-care reform, we will line up together behind you to make that happen."

In that moment, I realized that the way that we were funding community organizing, not just at Headwaters but at most foundations, was completely wrong. We were funding organizations that were working on important issues, but each of them was going their own way to solve that issue. There wasn't any larger momentum being developed, and as funders, we were encouraging a fracturing of movements.

As a result of this new thinking, just as things were at their darkest, something amazing happened. After we talked to the nonprofits we supported about lining up, they started working together differently. They saw each other as critical allies rather than competition for scarce resources. As a foundation, we adjusted our fundraising strategy to begin doing more grantmaking and program management for larger foundations that were interested in funding organizing groups, and extended our vision of who could be a donor to include young people and people of color. As a result of all of these changes, we were able to get more grant dollars to community-led groups, and the groups were able to more successfully utilize those resources by working collaboratively.

When I left Headwaters in 2013, our grantees had just finished a successful legislative session that culminated with the passing of ten bills that seemed impossible even a few years ago. Those bills included the legalization of gay marriage and the passage of a homeowners' bill of rights moved forward by an offshoot of the Occupy movement. These under-resourced community organizations were at the front line of a complete restructuring of American society.

There was a lot of trial and error in my five years leading the Headwaters Foundation, but I believe we developed an important model for taking advantage of current conditions and developing a clear vision for the future. Early in this crisis, I wished that I had a crystal ball to help me understand what to do next. The world was so different than my expectations, and the pace of change was faster than I'd ever had to deal with in my professional career. I realized most of the tools I had been taught in graduate school about nonprofit management were not useful in times of wholesale societal upheaval.

My Journey to the Future

Since that market drop in 2008, I have been on my own journey to learn as much as I can about the future. I've devoured too many hours of TED Talks to count; found comic strips from the 1950s and '60s about exciting advances that could come in the future; interviewed experts in dozens of fields including philanthropy, human genome mapping, disaster first response, self-driving cars, virtual reality, impact investing, community building, and asteroid mining; explored Afrofuturism; studied strategic foresight at Oxford; learned about the future of politics in Aspen; met with futurists at Disney; worked to create the future of philanthropy in Barcelona; learned about the value of human existence outside of work from a philosopher/cab driver in Iceland; spent time at the United Nations to learn about humanitarian challenges and opportunities; talked with the founders of Facebook, Virgin Galactic, Taser International (now Axon), the Center for Courage and Renewal, and Human Longevity, Inc., to learn how they are building a more positive future; and even stalked a billionaire who I believe has a unique perspective on what's coming next (more on that later). I did all of this because I wanted the future to be clearer for you than it was for me.

Starting my journey into futurism was intimidating. In most spaces, I was the only woman, the only person of color, and the only person under fifty. For a long time, I was also the only person from the social sector. In these spaces, the participants were developing relationships and making decisions that would impact our country and world for the next fifty years. But as I got more experienced and comfortable in the spaces, I stopped being intimidated and realized that they needed people like me.

The goal of futurism is to improve the future through better decision-making. But you can't make good decisions if you don't have a wide variety of perspectives. These blind spots make you miss unintended consequences, untapped resources, and new ideas to make the future better.

Why I Wrote This Book

Government, the military, and the private sector have all used the powerful tools of futurism extensively to strengthen their ability to understand what is coming next. I think it is time that we take advantage of those same tools to strengthen our work of making the world a better place, and I would love for us to be an active voice in the spaces and places where the future is being created.

I wrote this book to help fill in the gaps of our collective knowledge about what to do with uncertainty about the future. I skipped the technical and academic jargon to make this book accessible to people who care about making our communities better.

I wrote this book because I want you to join me on this journey to create the future.

What Are Futurism and Foresight?

First of all, there isn't a single, predetermined future; there are many possible futures determined by the decisions that we make today. Futurists are not creating an exact model of the future. We are using trends to determine what is possible, probable, and preferable in the future. We also analyze "wild cards," which are low-probability, high-impact events. Examples of wild cards are things like a major asteroid hitting Earth, communications satellites breaking down, or nuclear war.

Futurists use foresight, which is the ability to recognize patterns in the present and at the same time think about how those patterns will impact the future. Forecasting will not give you Nostradamus-like skills to predict that on January 5, 2030, the world's water crisis will end. Instead, they allow you to recognize which trends are emerging and to make the right step at an appropriate time to take advantage of or combat that trend. Using these skills allows you to develop successful long-term strategies and be well prepared for likely contingencies. This book will help you develop these foresight skills.

The Case for Using Futurism in Your Work

Traditionally, futurism has been used by two main groups. The first is businesses that are analyzing trends to get a competitive advantage and to understand what their customers might want in the future. One company that has been using futurism for a long time is the Shell Oil Company. Since the 1970s, the team at Shell Scenarios has been developing possible visions of the future to help leaders at the company explore how to move forward and make better decisions.

In 2008, the team at Shell Scenarios identified three hard truths:
1. A huge increase in global energy use is coming.
2. There won't be enough energy to keep up.
3. Climate change is real and getting worse.

This was the message from an *oil* company that didn't seem to have a vested interest in the public being outraged about climate change.

They developed two possible scenarios to address these challenges. In the first, which was called Blueprints, we get ahead of climate change and grassroots demands for carbon reduction make politicians move to action. In this scenario, global leaders develop a meaningful carbon-trading framework.

In the second possible scenario, Scramble, we get stuck in ideological differences. Some refuse to believe in climate change, and national governments have no appetite for curbing growth. This leads to runaway carbon pollution. It is too late to curb emissions, and we can only adapt to what the world becomes.

After these scenarios were complete, Shell Oil recommended the Blueprints option and asked governments to set carbon limits. Other big oil companies followed suit. Unfortunately, governments did not act meaningfully, and now we are living in the Scramble scenario.

The second primary audience for futurism is the federal government and, more specifically, the military. The Pentagon has a secretive Office of Net Assessment, which tries to anticipate future needs by developing scenarios and hosting war games—exercises that help to develop and refine military strategies. This office was created in 1973 to serve as the Pentagon's internal think tank to look twenty to thirty years into the military's future and identify threats and opportunities.

At the first futurism conference that I attended, I was shocked at how many participants worked directly for the US military or for one of their consulting firms. I asked one of the military contractors why futurism was important for the military, and he said, "We have to figure out who is going to hate us next, and futurism helps with that."

During my first few years learning about futurism, I was shocked at how few people from the social sector I saw at conferences and trainings. I could immediately see how helpful the tools that I was learning would be for my work.

Nonprofits, foundations, and social purpose businesses are working to solve some of society's toughest challenges. But by ignoring the tools of futurism, we are not using all of the tools at our disposal. We have a critical role in seeing what is coming next, not because we are trying to maximize our profits or figure out who is going to hate us next but because we are working on solutions to critical community issues.

Here are some ways having a future-focused lens could benefit the social sector:

- An international NGO brings donors into a refugee camp using virtual reality technology. Donors feel like they are actually in the camp and virtually meet some of the residents. They are more empathetic to a complicated refugee crisis because they feel like they have been there. Donors write bigger checks and the NGO can eliminate expensive and sometimes dangerous site visits for foundations and major donors.

- A grassroots neighborhood organization uses sophisticated online maps of projected sea-level rises to organize individual residents whose homes will be impacted by the changes. Those residents pressure elected officials to prioritize environmental solutions.

- A health foundation harnesses the power of low-cost drones to deliver lifesaving vaccines to communities without reliable road access.

- A social network uses blockchain technology to build a donation platform that transfers gifts from individual donors to nonprofit organizations with no transaction fees and full transparency on where the gifts come from and how they are used.

- A neighborhood association creates a tool-sharing service for residents in a three-block area that uses RFID trackers, a virtual asset tracker platform, and a messaging service to identify where tools are located for quick sharing.

- A school district creates a robust, AI-powered online learning system to supplement classroom education and to replace in-person learning when extreme weather prevents students from safely attending school.

- An international disaster-relief organization uses drones equipped with high-tech 3D mapping capabilities to safely access whole communities after a natural disaster and to alert local authorities to which roads are blocked or which buildings have collapsed. Heat-mapping technology is used to identify where potential victims might be located.

- A social purpose health-care business invests in creating low-cost DNA diagnostic tools that can identify cancer when it is at stage zero and most susceptible to treatment.

Becoming a future-focused leader allows you to:

- Focus your limited attention on the issues and strategies where you can have the largest impact, helping you create greater change on the issues that you are passionate about.
- Help others see a clear path forward on issues where there may not have been consensus before by crafting a vision of long-term success that people can buy into.
- Become more valuable to your organization and more marketable for future positions.

The Idea in Action

A few years ago, I went with my husband to run errands at Best Buy and was captivated by a new security system that was on sale. The system included a camera in your peephole so you could see who was knocking through a video feed on your phone, and you could remotely unlock the door from anywhere in the world through an app. You could let in your dog-walker or your neighbor who was watering your plants while you were out of town. My husband went to find what he needed, and when he came back twenty minutes later, I was still standing in front of the display. He was a little confused and asked me if we needed a security system. I said that we didn't. So he asked why I was still standing there. I told him I didn't realize that all of these individual technologies existed and that they had been under development for so long that they were now combined into one system that was on sale for ninety-nine dollars at Best Buy. As a futurist, I pay close attention to trends and emerging technologies, and at least weekly I am shocked by a new innovation. The purpose of paying attention to the future isn't so that you know exactly what is going to happen and when—it is that you have an idea of how to change what you do today to make tomorrow better.

Go Do It!

A few ideas on how to read this book:
- **Start with an open mind.** Some of the ideas in this book may feel far-fetched, and that's okay. We aren't used to thinking about the future, so this may feel out of your comfort zone. Take this opportunity to stretch your thinking.
- **You don't have to get it all right.** Understanding futurism isn't about predicting exactly what the future will look like. It's

about learning how to use tools that will help you better understand what's next.

- **Try it out.** This isn't a book about theory. It's full of stories from people in lots of sectors that have tried new tools and new ways to influence the future. In each chapter, find an idea or two that you can implement in your own work.

FutureGood All-Star:
Sir Richard Branson, Virgin Companies

Earlier in this chapter, I said that I stalked a certain billionaire. That billionaire was Sir Richard Branson. For many years, I have been impressed with how he takes big risks with his philanthropy and tackles many significant challenges. He describes himself as a serial philanthropist. He has made efforts to clean the ocean, to decriminalize drug use and treat it as a health problem, and to end global conflict using a group of world leaders called the Elders. Members of the Elders have included Nelson Mandela, Kofi Annan, and former president Jimmy Carter. These leaders, with trusted moral authority, are sent to places of global conflict to manage the mediation process.

Richard is a walking, breathing signal of the future philanthropy. The same entrepreneurial spirit that grew Virgin Companies from *Student* magazine to a four-hundred-company juggernaut is now being used to identify solutions for humanity's toughest challenges. I tried to find more information about how he was approaching his philanthropy, but I wasn't able to find many interviews where he described his philanthropic philosophy. When reporters were able to interview him, they were much more interested in how he got so rich or the thought behind his latest publicity stunt.

So I set a goal to interview him myself. It took a year of watching where he was scheduled to speak and working any relationship that I had to his company or foundation, but I was finally able to identify a time when he was speaking to a philanthropy association that I had close ties to. Using relationships, credibility I have built in my field, and sheer determination, I was able to finagle my way into a fifteen-minute private interview with him.

Here's what I learned from that interview (which you can find by googling Trista Harris and Richard Branson):

- **Take big bets.** Richard took bold chances in business, and he thinks it is irresponsible for people with access to wealth to not take similar bets to solve challenges in the world.
- **Use lobbying as a tool.** Many issues—like the environment, eliminating the death penalty, and decriminalizing drug addiction—take government action to create real change. Richard hasn't shied away from pressuring government to move on the issues he cares about.
- **Leverage cross-sector partnerships.** As someone who owns a variety of companies, he has been strategic to leverage his companies to work on the issues that he is passionate about on the philanthropic side. An example of this is when, in 2005, he pledged 100 percent of the proceeds from his transportation companies to alleviate global warming and to identify alternative sources of fuel. He is also working on figuring out how to run his airplanes on 100-percent alternative fuels. This process is tougher than traditional business, but it has a larger positive effect. He thinks that entrepreneurs can be successful while still contributing to the greater good.
- **Create room for others to align with your big vision.** Richard doesn't want to be the only or even the biggest donor at the table. He has used his private retreat, Necker Island, as a gathering place where he brings together philanthropists to encourage them to work on bigger issues together.

A few months after that amazing interview, I got an unexpected invitation to join a conference on the convergence of future technologies that was happening on Necker Island. I was able to present on the future of doing good and spend time with a group of extraordinary technologists, entrepreneurs, scientists, and Sir Richard Branson himself. During that trip, I was able to see how Richard has used his island to live his environmental mission. In just one of many examples, in the early 2000s he reintroduced thirty flamingos to the British Virgin Islands, where they haven't existed for the last hundred years. Now there are 150 new baby flamingos born each year in the islands.

As I was leaving the island, I had the most surreal experience. The boat that I was leaving on stopped; the driver said, "I don't want to hit my boss with the boat." I looked ahead and saw Sir Richard Branson wearing a full tuxedo, kitesurfing in the ocean ahead of us. As he zigzagged back and forth, we got a chance to speed ahead of him. As I looked back, he let go of the kite with one hand and waved to me as I left. It was then that I saw the photographer on the beach, who was shooting him kitesurfing for a photo spread.

I'm not telling you this story because it is the coolest thing that has happened to me. (It was.) I'm sharing this because sometimes you can create the future that you want for yourself by having a clear vision of what success looks like. Once I knew that success was connecting personally with Sir Richard Branson and learning as much as I could about his philanthropy, I noticed all of the opportunities that would make that future possible. I think it will work the same for you. As you get clearer about the future you are working to create for yourself and the issues that you care about, you start noticing opportunities and making decisions today that will make that future possible. That is the real benefit of having a future-focused mindset.

What is the big vision that you can set for yourself?

CHAPTER 01:

STOP, LOOK, GO MODEL

The future belongs to those who prepare for it today.
—Malcolm X

The social sector has two critical roles in our society. The first is to act as our collective safety net. Without our strong nonprofit sector, millions of American families would be without a roof over their heads or a meal in their stomachs. Whether or not you believe this is an appropriate role for the nonprofit sector or that the most basic of human needs are the responsibility of the government, the fact remains that, increasingly, nonprofits have been tasked with this responsibility. The second role of the social sector is to help civilization reach its collective potential. Investing in the arts, creating the tools for collective civic engagement, and exposing youth to new ideas rarely generate an immediate profit in the open market, but they are critical to our evolution as a species.

Nonprofits and foundations don't have a monopoly on creating a better future for our communities. There is also a bourgeoning interest in the private sector to make solving social problems a part of the business plan. Elon Musk is a great example of this trend. He didn't start Tesla because he was interested in running a car company; he started Tesla because he was concerned about global warming and believed that reengineering cars would have a great impact on the environment.

Even for companies that didn't start with a social purpose, there is an incentive in building a better future. Consumers are becoming much more selective and are willing to spend more money with companies that they believe match their values and are improving the world in some way. Companies have noticed this trend and are moving their corporate social-responsibility work out of the shadows, instead making it marketing-ready.

As a society, we can't afford for people who are working to make the world a better place to be using yesterday's information to solve tomorrow's problems. To address this and to help you understand and shape the future, I've created a model called Stop, Look, and Go.

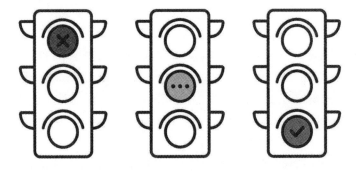

I created this model because I was frustrated in my own efforts to find a version of futurism that both worked for people trying to solve social issues and was easy enough for practitioners, not just paid futurist consultants, to undertake. Stop, Look, and Go is deceptively simple, but when used consistently, it can help you reshape your organization and the issues that you care about, creating a more abundant future. Each step of the framework is described in a few chapters of the book.

STOP

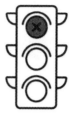

The first step is Stop. Stop is about ideas and ways of thinking that you have to let go of to better see the future. In the Stop chapters, you'll learn to stop believing the future is outside of your control, stop loving the problem, and stop thinking linearly.

LOOK

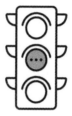

The second step is Look. Look is about noticing future trends and developing systems to keep track of those trends so they can inform your strategy. In the Look chapters, you'll be asked to look at your mindset, look for the clues that today gives us about tomorrow, and engage in scenario planning.

GO

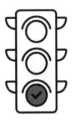

The third step is Go. Go is about putting what you have learned into action. In the Go chapters, you'll learn to develop a positive vision, develop a future-focused organization, and be a part of the FutureGood movement.

Here's how I have implemented the Stop, Look, Go framework in my own life.

Stop

Working on my mindset has been a continuous process. It isn't like I just decided one day to be more future-focused and then was suddenly there. I needed to notice my mindset and listen for times that I was loving the problem or unable to see exponential possibilities. The biggest tool for me in changing my mindset has been meditation. Meditation gives me the mental space to examine my thinking in a new way and to create the space for new ideas. I was only able to start meditating consistently after reading Hal Elrod's book *The Miracle Morning*, which is about changing your morning routine to have a better start to your day. You can take as much time as you would like to complete the steps of the miracle morning process, but it can be done in as little as six minutes. Here are the six steps of a miracle morning:

6 MINUTE MIRACLE MORNING

SILENCE
Sit calmly and peacefully. Breathe deeply and meditate or just sit in silence.

AFFIRMATIONS
Think of a short statement that reminds you of your purpose and repeat that to yourself.

VISUALIZATION
Visualize what your ideal day will look like with as much detail as possible. As an alternative visualize that your life would look like if you fully reach your purpose.

EXERCISE
Get your heart rate up. Move. Do jumping jacks. Anything that gets your blood pumping.

READING
Read a page or two from a book or a story that inspires you or helps you grow in some way.

SCRIBING
Take your journal and write down what your grateful for, what you are proud of, and what you plan to accomplish with your day.

Giving yourself room to start your day in a way that helps you stretch and grow gives you the space to be more future-focused.

Look

I've made the future a consistent part of my present. I set aside at least two hours a week, preferably in one block of time, to think about the future. I use this time to read interesting articles, brainstorm future conditions and possible strategies to react to those conditions, and write about the future for my organization's membership and for readers at my website.

I have Google alerts set for things like "the future of philanthropy," "future nonprofit," and "city of the future." These alerts help curate the types of articles I'm reading during my two hours. I also get regular email updates from Singularity University, a think tank focused on creating a more abundant future; Institute for the Future, a nonprofit strategic futures organization; the Future Today Institute, a foresight and strategy firm that helps leaders prepare for complex futures; and PolicyLink, a national research and action institute advancing racial and economic equity.

Having a steady stream of future-looking information helps me look beyond the present. If you'd like to receive some of my updates about the future of doing good, sign up at my website, TristaHarris.org.

The next part of my Look practices is to keep track of what I am noticing about the future. (More about this practice in chapter 6.) I use the app Evernote to keep track of future trends, clipping articles of interest and taking pictures of the journals that I brainstorm in and saving that information in Evernote. About once a month, I will look across many of the notes that I have kept in the app to see if there is a larger trend hidden in those details. I also try to think about how multiple trends might intersect with each other, like a growing hunger for human connection and more people working from home. Natural results of those two trends would be things like the rise of coworking spaces and people looking for retreats where they are connected to a community.

Go

The Go step has two main challenges: getting other people on board and managing your own instincts to stifle change or procrastinate.

There are a few things that I do to help other people get on board with change. I make sure that I bring stakeholders along throughout the process of understanding what is next, from the identification of the problems, to the design, to the implementation and the evaluation and revisions. Many people trying to implement change in an organization bring stakeholders together too late, right when the changes take effect. You need people invested throughout the process to build trust and momentum.

Managing your own impulses to stifle change or procrastinate can be more difficult because they are human instincts. Procrastination is not about your work ethic or competence; it is actually a behavior meant to help you cope with stress. If you are stressed, it makes sense to try to escape the thing that is stressing you out. That's great in the short-term, but it prevents you from growing and innovating.

Mel Robbins, author of *The 5 Second Rule*, has two critical steps to fighting this instinct:

1. The very first thing to do is to acknowledge that you're stressed. Don't analyze or dissect it. Just accept that what you're dealing with is not a fault, defect, or inability in you but a reaction to stress. It's real, and it's driving your decisions. That takes a bit

of the pressure off and enables your prefrontal cortex to play a role in the next decision.

2. Instead of trying to rationalize the stress, just count backward from five. When you get to one, spend five minutes doing the thing that is stressing you out instead of procrastinating. Make the call to your boss, write the email to the angry community member, write the next paragraph in your implementation plan. You break that cycle of procrastination and start moving forward. That momentum is critical to your success.

I use the five-second rule when I have a call I am dreading making, when I get stuck writing, and when I need to get a new person engaged in a project that I am excited about. It helps me to get out of my head and move to action.

Go Do It!

A few ideas on how to implement the Stop, Look, and Go steps:

*   **Upgrade your morning.** Try doing the Miracle Morning steps for two weeks. During your journaling, keep track of how your mindset is changing. Are you approaching your day with a more positive lens? Are you noticing more opportunities to improve the future?
*   **Look for the future in your inbox.** Set up Google alerts about the future of issues you care about, subscribe to blogs about the future, and start following people who care about the future on Twitter.
*   **Move past procrastination.** Think about what things are holding you back when it comes to implementing a new idea to improve the future. Use Mel Robbins's five-second rule to help you push through to action.

FutureGood All-Star:

Obi Felton, director of getting moonshots ready for contact with the real world at X

I met Obi Felton at Amy Webb's Future History Festival. I was blown away not just by Obi's cool job, but also how she approaches the work.

Obi Felten is one of the top executives at Alphabet's research arm, X, formerly known as Google X. This is the place where this tech juggernaut envisions its "moonshots": ambitious projects that aim to solve major world problems with cutting-edge technology. Impressive moonshot projects include Project Loon, which wants to provide internet connectivity to rural and remote areas of the world using balloons; Project Wing, which uses unmanned aerial flights for deliveries; and Waymo, Google's self-driving car company.

Most people run away from large, complex problems because they are risky and expensive to solve. Obi encourages her team to "run toward the monsters" because that's where the biggest rewards come from. She also encourages her team to spend a lot of time up front defining the problem and spending time with people that are impacted by it. She says that, traditionally, "We reward people for problem-solving rather than problem-stating."

Obi and the rest of the team at Alphabet understand that making the world a better place should be a critical part of their mission. "The idea of changing the world isn't at odds with making a buck," Felten said. In fact, the latter is usually necessary. "If you want to solve really large problems in the world, unless it's a sustainable business, it probably won't scale," she said. "So finding those things where there's both profit and purpose is sort of our sweet spot."

What are the big, monster problems you can tackle?

CHAPTER 02:

STOP BELIEVING THE FUTURE IS OUTSIDE OF YOUR CONTROL

"A society grows great when old men plant trees whose shade they know they shall never sit in."

—Greek Proverb

As a society, we used to get excited about the future. The space program, modernist design, even the cartoon *The Jetsons* made us feel like a more positive future was just around the corner. Kennedy's call for America to go to the moon inspired a whole generation of children to study science in the hopes that they would be a part of creating a multi-planet future for humanity. Over the last few decades, we have gotten more pessimistic about the future. As we get closer to the Jetsons' utopia (smart homes and Roombas are just the beginning), we seem to be buying into a vision of a dystopian future. I think popular media is partly to blame for this switch. We moved from *The Jetsons* to *WALL-E*, in which the planet was covered with garbage. We also have series like *The Matrix*, *Terminator*, and *The Hunger Games* feeding into the narrative that the future is something terrible right around the corner that we need to delay for as long as possible.

Even at the top levels of the social sector, this feeling is rampant. According to surveys and interviews conducted by the Center for Effective Philanthropy, of more than two hundred CEOs of the nation's biggest foundations only 1 percent felt that foundations were "very prepared" to deal effectively with coming changes in society, and only 13 percent believed that their foundations were making a significant difference in society. 98 percent of those CEOs said that foundations needed to change to address society's needs, but only 14 percent believe such change is "very likely." This is coming from the people in charge of the largest foundations in the country, who arguably have nothing but time, resources, and space to create the changes that they bemoan are not happening.

This is nonsense. The future is not out of our control. It is determined by the choices that we make today. When it comes to the future, we don't have a resource gap or a good idea gap; we have a belief gap.

To begin rethinking our relationship with the future in a more productive and empowering way, here are some places to start:

Look to the past to identify the success stories. Find examples of people throughout history that have worked on your issue and have had long-term impact. What were their methods, how did they introduce their innovations, and what progress was made? Learn from that history.

For example, Martin Luther King, Jr., studied how Mahatma Gandhi used nonviolence as a political tool to oust the colonial powerhouse Great Britain from India. Gandhi understood the ties of oppression between African Americans and Indians under colonialism. He met with a group of African American leaders visiting India in 1935, including Benjamin Mayes, who became president of Morehouse College in Atlanta, which King attended.

As a mentor to King, Mayes encouraged him to read Gandhi's writing. King later wrote that Gandhi's teachings were "the guiding light of our technique of nonviolent social change," which not only effectively mobilized hundreds of thousands of people but also set the conditions for civil rights activists and lawyers to fight for racial equity within the framework of the justice system. During a 1959 visit to India, King said, "To other countries I may go as a tourist, but to India I come as a pilgrim."

Who has created significant change on an issue that is important to you? They may be in a different community or country or may have lived during another era, but learning how they thought and created change can inform your work moving forward.

Identify the future-focused outliers (the utopists). Who is looking at the future of your issue? Who are the big thinkers? What are the big ideas? Do any of those excite you? Why?

Here are some places to look for these future-focused leaders:

- Who are the most exciting keynotes at industry conferences that you attend? Are they saying something that is different from the commonly accepted knowledge on the issue that you care about?
- TED Talks are a great place to find new ideas. Has someone spoken about your issue, or does someone have a talk about another issue that gives you a new way to think about what you care about? For example, maybe Bill Strickland's talk on building a neighborhood with beauty, dignity, and hope will give you a new perspective on your own community development efforts. Or maybe Steven Strogatz's talk on how flocks of birds and fish manage to synchronize and act as a unit when no one is giving orders will help you develop a new strategy for community organizing.

- Who is promoting solutions that are the exact opposite of your thinking on an issue? Deeply investigate their thinking and see if there is something to learn from their perspective.
- Google search the future of education, or economic development, or transportation. What do you find from people who are thinking twenty to fifty years forward on your issue?

Identify the nexus for action. Who are groups of people that are working together to improve the issue? Collective impact tables, which are just a group of important actors from different sectors with a commitment to a common agenda to solve a specific social problem at scale, have come into vogue. Find an effective collective impact table for the issue that you are passionate about.

StrivePartnership is considered an early leader in the collective-impact movement. Founded in 2006 by school administrators, college and university presidents, foundation leaders, corporate executives, and nonprofit directors from Cincinnati and Northern Kentucky, its participants share a commitment to a collective strategy to improve educational outcomes for children on both sides of the river from cradle to career. This model has been replicated by more than fifty communities across the country.

Over the first ten years, measurable improvements have been made in all six indicators along StrivePartnership's cradle-to-career continuum: kindergarten readiness, early-grade reading, middle-grade math, college/career readiness, college/career persistence, and career/life pursuit.

Despite this tremendous progress, the work of the StrivePartnership is not yet complete. Most notably, achievement levels for children of color and children from low-income homes and neighborhoods continue to be appreciably less than those of affluent, white children. As StrivePartnership continues its work, they have committed to advancing the next level of collective impact by fortifying the urban education ecosystem in Cincinnati and Northern Kentucky to ensure racial and economic equity. To do this, they will now include parents and caregivers, teachers, grassroots leaders, small business operators, and students themselves as critical stakeholders.

In this new, expanded model, they draw upon the insights and authority of these community-based stakeholders and actively enlist them in the codesign and coproduction of solutions. Together they are imagining and creating a more equitable future for their region's children.

Go Do It!

Here are some ways to stop believing the future is out of your control:

Spend time imagining what the issue that you care about would look like if it was fully fixed and no longer a problem. For example, if you are concerned about homelessness in your city, what would it look like if every single resident had housing? What would be different? How would that be operationalized?

You will probably start to think about all of the reasons that is impossible, and that's a good thing. You might think, "It is almost impossible to serve people who don't want to address their substance abuse issues or who don't want to be connected to social service programs." Start there, and develop a solution that would work best for that population. Maybe a tiny house model that uses public land. Maybe a wet house (alcohol allowed) model that provides the safety and security of a home, even if the participant is still using alcohol or drugs. What if the security of stable housing then creates the conditions where an individual can finally address their substance abuse issues? Starting with a vision of your preferred future will help you identify new solutions.

Find opportunities to see the future in action. The writer William Gibson said, "The future is already here—it just isn't evenly distributed." Is there a community or a program that has solved the problem that you are concerned with? Go visit them, in person or virtually. What have they learned during that process?

A few years ago, I took a group of young philanthropists of color to Barcelona to see what future-focused city design look like. Being in a place that has already implemented the innovations you'd like to see in your local community is a great way to stretch your thinking about what is possible.

Imagine your own future impact. How would you like to be remembered? What is the change that you would like to create? It is important to remember that your past impact doesn't have to be your future legacy.

In 2012, the singer, actor, and civil rights leader Harry Belafonte accused Beyoncé, as well as other Black artists, of being part of a generation of Black artists who have "turned their back on social responsibility." That could have been the end of the story, but in just a few short years since that indictment, Beyoncé has leveraged her enormous platform to lift up the Movement for Black Lives and draw attention to the crisis of officer-involved shootings. According to a 2016 *New York Times* article, "Beyoncé's activism has been more closely tied to her art. Early this year, she released 'Formation,' on which she sang intensely about Black beauty and cultural pride. In the video, a dancing Black boy induces a row of armed officers to raise their hands in surrender, and Beyoncé herself is draped atop a police cruiser as it sinks into the water. Her vigorous Super Bowl halftime show performance of the song included nods to the Black Panthers; it was the most widely seen act of political art in recent memory."

Beyoncé and her husband, Jay-Z, provided bail money for protesters in Ferguson and Baltimore after a call from activist dream hampton, who also wrote Jay-Z's 2010 biography, *Decoded*. dream wrote that police are "waging war on black resistance in a multitude of ways, many of them financially. Protest is literally punished with tariffs when they fine and arrest people for protesting, more opportunities for exploitation by the state are possible with each encounter." Beyoncé has learned how to leverage her voice to influence the future.

FutureGood All-Star:

Chris Hughes, cofounder of Facebook and founder of the Economic Security Project

Chris Hughes is a cofounder of Facebook and the author of *Fair Shot: Rethinking Inequality and How We Earn*. He is also founder of the Economic Security Project, a network of policymakers, academics, and technologists working to end poverty and rebuild the middle class. I had the chance to sit down with Chris and learn more about a solution that he is proposing: universal basic income.

Universal basic income (UBI) is a form of social security in which all citizens receive an unconditional sum of money from the government or another public institution. Universal income gives everyone enough money to meet their basic needs, thus providing an income floor. Income earned on top of basic income can be used to improve living conditions. Proponents say basic income could eliminate poverty and support entrepreneurship and creativity.

We are undergoing a rapid transformation. Automation is disrupting our economy, and communities of color and low-income communities are the first to feel this transformation. According to market research firm Forrester, by 2021 robots and artificial intelligence will eliminate 6 percent of all U.S. jobs. The transportation, logistics, and customer service industries will take the biggest hits initially, but automation will be felt across all fields in the not-too-distant future. Imagine dangerous jobs like mining and manufacturing, or monotonous positions such as those in call centers, replaced by robots able to work around the clock.

It's not just entry-levels jobs that will be lost. IBM's Watson supercomputer has already diagnosed complex medical conditions that human doctors couldn't, and lawyer bots have successfully

fought hundreds of thousands of traffic tickets in New York City
and elsewhere. Business will reap the benefits of the transition with
a smaller workforce and increased profits. But businesses need customers, and widespread unemployment will have a devastating effect on income. Today, the middle class spends a larger percentage
of its income on food, shopping, and consumables than the rich do.
In the future, when many remaining jobs are low-paid, if employees
combine salaries with UBI, they will rise to the middle class, and
business can continue to rely on their patronage.

Chris argues that automation and robotics are a part of the story
but aren't the full picture. "Jobs in America have already come
apart," he says. "That is one of the effects of automation, and globalization in particular: all of the jobs in the past 10 years that we've
created, 94 percent of them are part-time, contract, temporary, sea-
sonal. Yeah, unemployment is near a record low, but the jobs that
are out there are not providing the kind of 40-hours-a-week benefits
like sick leave or retirement benefits."

Universal and partial basic income programs have been tested
worldwide, and it turns out that giving people money is good for the
economy. In 2013, people in Indian villages who received payments
saw increased economic activity, higher work rates, and many more
people starting businesses. In 2008 Uganda, unconditional cash
transfers inspired economic growth, and a 2011 Kenyan trial found
higher rates of economic consumption.

Without UBI, high unemployment will lead to tremendous civil
unrest. We know that rising inequality leads to rising unrest, de-
pression, and community violence. UBI ensures that people's basic
needs are met, and trials report increased high school graduation
rates and lower rates in hospitalizations and crime. UBI gives people more time to care for children and elders, play active roles in
their communities, and help solve society's biggest challenges.

Chris proposes a simple solution: "We should provide a guaranteed income of $500 a month for every working adult who makes less than $50,000, paid for by raising taxes on the top 1 percent. A guaranteed income of this size would cut the number of people living in poverty in half and stabilize the financial lives of much of the middle class, for less than half of what we spend each year on defense."

What are the big societal shifts that you see that we need in the future?

CHAPTER 03:

STOP LOVING THE PROBLEM

*"We cannot solve our problems with the same thinking
we used when we created them."*

—Albert Einstein

In the social sector, we spend a ton of time loving the problem. We sit in meetings where we go through PowerPoints that describe how terrible a local neighborhood is with charts and graphs. Foundations ask nonprofits to describe the problem that they are working on, and funding is usually dependent on how dire you can make the problem seem. As a former problem-lover, I know the allure. We think that if people only understood how bad the problem was, they would do something different to fix it.

Years ago, I cochaired the African American Leadership Forum, a network of over a thousand African American leaders in Minnesota who were working together to develop a policy agenda to close the many racial disparities that we have in Minnesota. We hosted an event for foundation and nonprofit leaders to make the case for why they should care about the local African America community. We had one of our members do the Generic Disparities PowerPoint™. Your local community probably has its own version, but in Minnesota our slides said things like:

- Minnesota has one of the largest educational achievement gaps in the nation between Black students and White students.
- Our financial gap between Whites and people of color is the biggest in the nation.
- *POLITICO* article: "Something Is Rotten in the State of Minnesota."
- *MinnPost*: "Twin Cities' Persistent Racial Inequality Begins at Home."

I have presented the Generic Disparities PowerPoint™ many times myself and was really proud of the fact that I could clearly state the problem. My hope was that once decision-makers understood that there was a problem and how large it was, they would do *something* to make the problem better. At that time, I wasn't quite sure what the *something* was, but I believed it was outside of the scope of my presentation. I was making the case that people should care, and someone else was probably figuring out how to fix it.

On this fateful day, our special guest was the brilliant Angela Glover Blackwell. Angela is founder and chief executive officer of PolicyLink, a national research and action institute advancing economic and social equity. Her role at our event was to further make the case that there were problems impacting the African American community that needed fixing. Angela listened patiently to the Generic Disparities PowerPoint™ and then was introduced. When she got on the stage, the first thing she said was, "My mom taught me to be polite, so I didn't want to turn around and look at the audience while this lovely, smart woman was giving her presentation." She then pointed to the presenter of the Generic Disparities PowerPoint™. "But the whole time, I was wondering, *Aren't you embarrassed?*" She looked pointedly at the audience. "If

I lived here and someone described such big disparities that are determined by race, I would be embarrassed." The audience shifted uncomfortably in their seats. "My question is, what are you *doing* to close these gaps?" The discomfort in the audience was particularly strong because Minnesotans aren't used to very pointed questions, especially about race. More importantly, the disparities had felt to many people like something to be discovered and talked about, but we had not gotten to the fixing conversation.

Often conversations about disparities sounded like: "Did you know we have disparities?"

"Why, yes, I did know we had disparities, and here is an additional fact so that you understand that I understand that we have disparities."

People would nod knowingly to each other, secure in the feeling that they were both very knowledgeable about disparities, and then the cycle would continue.

While it is helpful to know the scope of the problem you are working on, the work can't stop there. Spending so much time describing the problem makes you feel like you have done something because you have used a lot of energy and time during that process. You are active, you are going to meetings, you are doing research. You are talking about critical issues with the right people. All of these things feel very important, but the mistake is believing that this is what will lead to change. Just talking about problems has never led to a breakthrough solution. You may also use up all of your energy and the will of your stakeholders describing how terrible things are rather than doing the hard work to fix the problem.

When Angela jolted us with her question, "Aren't you embarrassed?", it moved the conversation to a place of responsibility, which is a step you need to take to get to action.

Quite a few changes happened after Angela gave us a

community-wide epiphany. We stopped calling the gap between Black and White test scores an education gap and instead called it an opportunity gap. The issue was not that Black children were not as smart as White children; they just had fewer educational opportunities. We started to describe the sort of educational opportunities that we wanted to build for Black students.

We were able to move from *loving* the problem to actually *fixing* the problem.

Here are some skills you can develop to help you stop loving the problem:

Learn to skip the problem. Daniel Burrus is a talented futurist. His book *Flash Foresight* is one of the reasons I first became interested in futurism. He has a concept called "problem skipping," which I think is very helpful for reformed problem lovers. Daniel says that "every organization has problems, and often when you are trying to 'fix' a tough problem, the organization gets even more mired in the challenge and can't get past the roadblock. A better solution to solving those tough problems is to just skip them. When you confront your roadblock by leaping over it rather than having it stop you from reaching your goals, you see new solutions you never knew existed."

Here are some ways that you can start to skip the problem:

Find the real problem that is buried. Most problems are complex and are composed of multiple smaller problems. As you start to pull apart the problem that you are working on and look at it from multiple angles, you may find that the problem you had been focused on wasn't the one causing you the pain.

Go away from the crowd. Sometimes, the opposite of what you perceive to be the problem is really your solution. For example, the common wisdom is that children need more classroom time to learn the material that is covered in standardized exams; now, think about how you could accomplish the same goals with *less* classroom time. Would children have longer recesses, more time in gym, more time in art class? Would spending time in those ways give children more ability to process what they had learned in the classroom and lower their stress level so that they were more relaxed during standardized tests? Digging deeper into the opposite of common wisdom may give you the transformative solution to solve the problem.

Technology opens new doors. Today's exponentially growing technology offers us new ways to solve old problems. Spend some time thinking about how emerging technology might give you a new option for solving a problem. How could mobile phones, artificial intelligence, drones, virtual reality, or robots be a useful tool?

For example, if you have ever bought a handmade Indian rug, it is likely that it was woven by children, many of whom are slaves. Activists that are working to end this child slavery crisis are excited about advances in robotic technology. If a robot could make a rug faster and cheaper than a child and could work twenty-four hours a day, that could make child slavery a less attractive option for factory owners.

Imagine what the problem would look like if it were fixed. I believe you can skip the problem by imagining what the world would look like if the problem that you cared about was completely fixed. Spending an exceptional amount of time imagining what success would look like might help you identify new solutions that are different than the sort of solutions you develop when you are trying to make a problem 5 percent better year after year. Completely fixing a problem often comes with a whole new set of solutions.

An interesting example of this is an offshoot of the prison reform movement that advocates for abolishing prisons altogether. Social activist Angela Davis says, "Mass incarceration is not a solution to unemployment, nor is it a solution to the vast array of social problems that are hidden away in a rapidly growing network of prisons and jails. However, the great majority of people have been tricked into believing in the efficacy of prisons, even though the historical record demonstrates that prisons do not work." When you start from the framework of eliminating an institution rather than merely reforming it, a whole new set of solutions is developed.

Imagine it this way: If prisons weren't an option, we would need to develop enhanced models of supervised release, community service, or restitution to victims. We would have to develop a new model of crime prevention rather than punishment. We could decriminalize drug use and instead develop a stronger system of drug treatment. Starting to think within a framework where prisons no longer exist suddenly gives you a new laundry list of solutions that you could start to implement now to improve the current prison system. Those ideas would be more impactful than the ideas that you would have developed if you started with the question of how you could make the current prison system better.

Take some time, not just once but often, to imagine what the world would look like if the problem that you cared about were fully solved.

Change your language. The language that you use determines how successful you will be at solving your issue. Often we get stuck in the rut of describing problems rather than focusing on solutions. In communications, there is a theory that suggests the way something is presented to the audience (called "the frame") influences the choices people make about how to process that information. Framing is the way the brain finds patterns in chaos and creates meaning out of lots of pieces of data. Frames can be a helpful shortcut, but they can also exacerbate biases and distort new solutions.

Trabian Shorter, founder and CEO of BMe, is addressing this issue head-on. Trabian wanted to change the narrative about Black men in the United States. He was sick of Black men being described as thugs, absentee fathers, and drains on society. He believed not only that that narrative was limiting the educational and employment opportunities of all Black men, but that it was also putting their lives at risk when police officers could only see them through that lens. When you only have a negative lens for a whole community, your frame starts to fill in details that aren't actually there. That is how a Black man holding a cellphone or a set of car keys in his backyard is perceived as a threat by a police officer and how that officer (and whole justice systems) justify shooting of unarmed Black men.

To address this issue, Trabian and BMe developed a model of asset framing that identifies people by their contributions rather than their costs. This frame then positions Black men as catalysts for community building and national social change, rather than a drain on society. Then they engage Black men to continue or begin to live out their aspirational identity. This is a big win for themselves and society. To do this, BMe connects Black male leaders with key influencers across industries and sectors who share their belief in valuing all members of the human family. BMe invites people of all races and genders to become involved as well by sharing BMe's uplifting content and participating in events and campaigns that create educated children, safer communities, healthier people, and economic opportunities—led by Black men.

When you frame the issue that you are passionate about, do you use language like *low-income, at-risk, marginalized, underserved,* or *achievement gap*? Reframe how you talk about the issue so that you are describing what you want, instead of what the problem is. This change will adjust the frame that you are using and will make it more likely that you will have the successful outcome that you desire.

Case Study: Infrastructure in Sub-Saharan Africa

Here's an example of loving the problem that Peter Diamandis of the X Prize Foundation often uses: Foundations and aid organizations were fretting over how to develop a telecommunications and electrical infrastructure for sub-Saharan Africa. That sort of infrastructure is unbelievably expensive to build and difficult to maintain, but it is critical for quality of life. It ensures that doctors and patients have a connection in very rural areas, it is needed for economic markets to work effectively, and it improves the ability of students to study and remain connected. There were conferences, grant initiatives, high-level talks with government officials, and a ton of circling around the problem of how to make that infrastructure possible, with no clear solution in sight and the cost of building infrastructure increasing each year.

With new technology, MTN Group completely skipped the problem. By providing solar chargers in the communities where they sold their phones, they allowed communities to have access to the benefits of significant telecommunications and electrical infrastructure without having to build that infrastructure. Peter says that today, a Masai man in Kenya with a smartphone "has access to more knowledge and information than the US president did just fifteen years ago."

People in places that previously didn't have telecommunications infrastructure now have access to:

- market pricing, so they can choose which market to sell their fish at based on who is the closest and paying the highest rate
- telemedicine, where a doctor that is located in a major city or even another country can speak with the patient via video chat and talk through treatment options
- GPS and more efficient travel
- free online classes at many of the world's top universities
- almost unlimited books and music
- the technology to produce content through video cameras and access the internet in ways that were impossible previously

This doesn't only benefit those previously unconnected communities; it benefits all of us. What will those newly connected billions of people have to add to our collective knowledge and understanding of people? What new solutions will they bring to previously unsolvable problems?

Go Do It!

Here are some ways to stop loving the problem:

- **Stop making the problem your guest of honor.** Stop hosting meetings where the sole purpose is to love the problem. Have a solutions mentality while you are planning events.
- **Check your communications.** Stop framing all of your grant applications and presentation around how terrible the problem is. Instead, move to a solutions frame.
- **Move the conversation.** If you are in a meeting where people

are spending a lot of time loving the problem, ask pointed questions about possible solutions to pivot the discussion.

FutureGood All-Star:
Majora Carter, founder of Majora Carter Group

Majora Carter is a trusted colleague and a hero of mine who has a gift for building a positive frame. I first learned about her work from her amazing TED Talk called "Greening the Ghetto," which was one of the first six available online. With her inspired ideas and fierce persistence, Carter managed to bring the South Bronx its first open-waterfront park in sixty years, Hunts Point Riverside Park. Then she scored $1.25 million in federal funds for a green-way along the South Bronx waterfront, bringing the neighborhood open space, pedestrian and bike paths, and space for mixed-use economic development in an area that was formerly a trash dump. Majora wasn't discouraged by the garbage-filled eyesore; she had the ability to imagine what was possible and brought the project to fruition by inspiring others with her dream.

I've gotten to know Majora personally through her work leading StartUp Box. This social enterprise is designed to increase opportunities for South Bronx community members to be a part of the tech economy by creating a technological and entrepreneurial ecosystem in the South Bronx. They create accessible on-ramps to tech jobs in the South Bronx through quality assurance (QA) as a subcontractor to NYC developers.

"StartUp Boxers" test games and other software across a range of devices and operating systems from start to finish, using industry protocols for bug reporting while gaining exposure to a wide range of product failures not normally observed by consumers. Teamwork is essential in tackling error-detection challenges across platforms, so communications, record keeping, and related team management skills are reinforced. Many tech service jobs, such as QA, provide earned income with a relatively short training period, and QA is a demonstrated entry-level position for many other opportunities in tech as well.

Where others saw unemployed troublemakers, Majora saw an untapped human resource that could be a benefit to the tech sector while providing new economic opportunities for community members. The result of this shift in framing is new jobs in an area that desperately needs them and a more diverse set of possible employees for a tech sector that has been having a hard time recruiting and retaining employees from diverse communities.

What is the untapped resource for the issue that you care about and how can you leverage that resource?

CHAPTER 04:

STOP LINEAR THINKING

"Exponential change runs counter-intuitive to the way that our linear brains make projections about change, and so we don't realize how fast the future is coming."

—Jason Silva

Human brains are programmed to predict the future. As we tracked an animal in the field, we could predict how far it would go based on its current speed and direction. We could estimate how long it would take us to get to a neighboring village based on how far we had already traveled. But the early human brain was not exposed to exponential change, and this is the challenge of our time. Peter Diamondis, CEO of the X Prize Foundation, describes it this way:

"As humans we evolved on this planet over the last hundreds of thousands of years in an environment that I would call local and linear. . . . The only things that affected you as you were growing up on the plains of Africa was what was in a day's walk. . . . Nothing changed generation to generation.

"Today we're living in a world that is exponential and global. Something happens in China or Korea, it affects you in Manhattan literally minutes later, through stock prices, news, whatever it might be. . . . The life of your grandparents, your parents, you, your kids is extraordinarily different in every possible way and we know this from going to Best Buy and finding a computer that is twice as fast or four times as fast for the same dollars as you bought it a year or two ago."

There is a fable that I think perfectly brings to life the idea of exponential growth:

Hundreds and hundreds of years ago, there was a King in India who loved to play games. But he had gotten bored of the games that were present at the time and wanted a new game that was much more challenging. He commissioned a poor mathematician who lived in his kingdom to come up with a new game.

After months of struggling with all kinds of ideas, the mathematician came up with the game of Chaturanga. The game had two armies, each led by a King who commanded the army to defeat the other by capturing the enemy King. It was played on a simple eight-by-eight square board.

The King loved this game so much that he offered to give the poor mathematician anything he wished for. "I would like one grain of rice for the first square of the board, two grains for the second, four grains for the third, and so on doubled for each of the sixty-four squares of the game board," said the mathematician.

"Is that all?" asked the King. "Why don't you ask for gold or silver coins instead of rice grains?"

"The rice should be sufficient for me," replied the mathematician. The King ordered his staff to lay down the grains of rice and soon learned that all the wealth in his kingdom would not be enough to buy the amount of rice needed on the sixty-fourth square. In fact, the whole kingdom's supply of rice was exhausted before the thirtieth square was reached. "You have provided me with such a great game and yet I cannot fulfill your simple wish. You are indeed a genius," said the King, and he offered to make the mathematician his top advisor instead.

When you look at the first rows of the chessboard, the amount of rice doesn't seem like such a big deal. This is the deceptive phase of exponential growth. It isn't until you get to the second half of the chessboard that the growth out of hand. This is the disruptive phase of growth. We have to develop our thinking to see exponential growth, even when it is very small and make decisions, before that growth becomes unimaginable.

You often hear about exponential growth as it pertains to technology. Moore's law refers to an observation made by Intel cofounder Gordon Moore in 1965 that the number of transistors per square inch on integrated circuits had doubled every year since their invention. Specifically, Moore's Law claims that CPU processing power will double approximately every two years for the price of $1,000. Ray Kurzweil took that observation to the next level in his book *The Law of Accelerating Returns*, where he described that this law of exponential growth in computing power also held for the mechanical computing devices of the 1890s, vacuum tube computers, and transistor-based machines.

I remember hearing news stories about LCD TVs in the 1990s where the newscasters were laughing because the TV cost $100,000. "Who needs a $100,000 television?" they asked. What they didn't realize is that the company manufacturing the TV understood that the cost and memory that powered the TV were going down exponentially, at a completely predictable pace. They were creating the TV and waiting for the memory cost to go down to match consumer spending, and that is exactly what happened.

There are many other things that are currently at the deceptive phase of development—like self-driving cars, AI on our phones, and robots in our workplaces—that feel like more of a pain or a fantasy than a benefit. But very quickly, these technologies will move from deceptive to disruptive to a variety of industries, including the social sector.

As future-focused leaders, it is critical that we understand what exponential growth looks like and what it means for the issues that we care about so that we can get ahead of a change before it moves from deceptive to disruptive.

A word of caution about humans and exponential growth:

Exponential growth also applies to changes in humanity. Our everyday lives used to be relatively easy to predict. Men had the careers that their father had. If you father was a blacksmith, you were a blacksmith, and you would teach your son to be a blacksmith. Women raised children and cared for the home. The blacksmith would live within fifty miles of his immediate family, and this wouldn't really change generation after generation. Teenagers could see broad strokes of their own lives by looking at their parents.

Compare that to now. My life as a college student in the late '90s was completely different from the life I live today. I used to walk across campus and put my name on a list to use a computer to access email. Most of my research still involved physical books, and if I wanted to make plans with friends, we had all better show up at the correct time and place; otherwise, there would be no way to reach each other.

Today I work collaboratively with people from around the world. We can edit the same document, talk in real time over Skype, and have access to a world of information on our phones—all for free once we have the hardware. My husband and I used to playfully argue over pop culture facts; now when we disagree, it only takes him a second to ask, "Siri, how old is Martha Stewart?" I have had my genome sequenced and found out that I need more vitamin D and that my preferred method of exercise should be long-distance running. (I don't care what you say, DNA test. I'm still not running a marathon.)

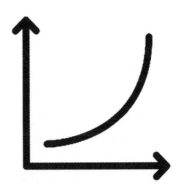

This pace of change in what my day-to-day life looks is at the knee of the exponential curve. But, because our brain is wired for the linear change that the blacksmith experienced, humans revert to what is most comfortable during times of extreme growth. Babies are the most visible example of this. When my son was small, he went from sleeping through the night and being a generally happy little guy to waking up three or four times during the night and being a screaming mess when he was awake. My husband and I were exhausted, and I asked my daycare provider what the heck was going on. She said that when babies are developing new skills, they revert to an earlier developmental stage before they take the leap. A few weeks later, he began walking and started to sleep through the night again.

Adults often share this pattern. As we grapple with the changes that technological advances have brought to our workplaces and our economy, some people revert back to old ideas of racism and nationalism as a security blanket for growth that they don't yet understand. It is easier to blame immigrants and people of color for job losses when you don't understand how robotics and artificial intelligence are impacting your job security. We are holding onto old ideas because we don't understand the future and because change, especially exponential change, is hard.

As people who do good for a living, it is our responsibility to help people in our communities understand what technology changes will mean for their day-to-day lives so that they can better see the exponential change that is impacting them, rather than just feeling that change, not understanding it, and lashing out like that screaming baby.

Dan Sullivan from The Strategic Coach has developed a model of societal transformation that clearly describes this time of exponential change that we are living through. Dan describes how society has always had three main stabilizers and accelerators. Traditionally, religious groups, government, and families act as stabilizing forces in society. Finance, science, and technology are the accelerating forces. Stabilizing forces are necessary because they give people something consistent to hold on to during periods of rapid change. Accelerating forces are necessary for progress and prevent us from getting too stagnant.

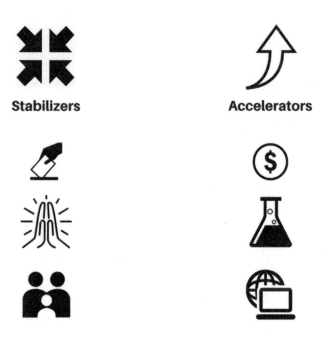

Stabilizers

- Political systems offer continual societal adjustments and improvements, ideally without violence and destruction.
- Religion creates unifying moral and ethical frameworks for greater cooperation within groups.
- Family favors genetically linked individuals with exclusive support, advantages, and opportunities.

Accelerators

- Financial incentives increase expansion of economic cooperation and competition across political borders.

- Science transforms natural processes and forces into usefully predictable formulas.
- Technology endlessly combines existing capabilities into unpredictably better capabilities.

The huge challenge for us today is that all of the forces that have historically acted as stabilizers are unstable. Our political institutions, both in the United States and around the world, are becoming more and more unpredictable. President Trump's win was a complete shock to traditional political pundits. Trump was able to harness the discontent of a chunk of society that was frustrated with the current pace of change and longed for a leader who promised a return to simpler times. The Brexit movement in Britain, a 2016 voter referendum to exit the European Union, was successful because of a similar feeling.

Some of our religious institutions are not fulfilling their role of being the keeper of moral frameworks. Sexual misconduct, financial embezzlement, prioritizing political power building over spiritual guidance, and religious terrorism are leading to a distrust in religious institutions. While Americans are still more religious than most of their counterparts in the rest of the Western world, according to a Gallup poll, just 44 percent of Americans have a great deal of trust in the church or organized religion.

Families have always been the bedrock of human society. Traditionally geographically close, families would share land and resources to make sure that their genetically connected people would have advantages and their genes would persevere. Now, as we move to a more global workforce, extended families are often no longer geographically connected. Your child might go away for college in California, marry someone from Kenya, and take a job in Switzerland.

Since we are living through a time where our stabilizing forces have become less stable and our accelerating forces are moving at an exponential pace, a critical role for the social sector is to reinforce our stabilizing institutions so they can be our bedrock during this time of change. If we don't support these institutions, people start to try to slow down or destroy the accelerators—and each other. You can push people to a certain point of progress, but they will usually snap back to their comfort point.

A few suggestions to help us through this transition by strengthening our stabilizing forces in society:

Hyperlocal politics bridge the gap. As people feel more and more disconnected from the federal government and like the federal government does not understand their local concerns and needs, there is a need for reinvestment in hyperlocal government. People want their government institutions to be personal and immediate. Government has to understand the day-to-day needs of its constituents and adjust its services to meet their unique needs.

To make hyperlocal politics more representative, work to elect local candidates who share your values and who reinforce stability in government through the respect of the rule of law and a commitment to transparency. Use your voice and resources to invest in a new generation of politicians who are diverse, engaged, and ready to make our communities better. Spending more time and energy on local changes will have a positive impact on the strength and vitality of our local communities.

An example of this type of leader is Ilhan Omar. Ilhan was born in 1982 in Mogadishu, Somalia. Her mother died when she was a child, so she was raised by her father, who worked as a teacher trainer, and her grandfather, who was director of Somalia's National Marine Transport. The family had to leave Somalia during the civil war, and Ilhan ended up in a Kenyan refugee camp, where she lived for four years. The family emigrated to the United States, and she quickly learned English. Her father and her grandfather taught her the importance of democracy, and at fourteen years old, she began to accompany her grandfather to caucus meetings to act as his interpreter.

On the same night that Donald Trump was elected president, Ilhan Omar was elected to the Minnesota House of Representatives as the first Somali-American legislator in the United States. Ilhan became a glimmer of hope for those who were pushing against the politics of division. She was elected by increasing voter turnout by over 30 percent and unseating a forty-four-year incumbent.

Ilhan's background as a refugee who fled political persecution has strengthened her resolve to uphold democratic norms. She says, "When you experience that kind of instability, you really appreciate and want to work hard to live in an environment that is free of that. I grew up under a dictatorship. I knew what it meant for people to not have the ability to freely express themselves. For my father and grandfather, the idea of coming to the United States and living under a democracy meant that they would have the freedoms of liberty, and justice for all would be extended to them, and that it would be extended to their children. I want to make sure that these ideals and the legacy that our country is supposed to uphold, does so."

Be a part of a group with clear moral and ethical frameworks (religious or not) and hold our institutions accountable for shared moral frameworks. Historically religion has been a critical stabilizing force in our society because it lays out a shared framework for what is right and what is wrong. Our society has started to lose trust in religious institutions, and we need to rebuild frameworks within some religious institutions that have lost their way and identify

other organizations that can be a stand-in for those religious institutions. For example, both nonprofits and businesses with a strong,
authentic, and transparent moral framework will be more likely to
receive support in the future because they will fulfill our need for
stability.

As an individual, take time to understand your own values
around what is right and wrong, and then identify organizations
and communities that share those beliefs.

Build close relationships with family (genetic or chosen) and
constantly lift up and support them. As families become more
geographically distant and decrease in size, we need to fill this
important gap that provides a personally stabilizing force for us.

One of the future-focused thinkers that I have been watching is
Mia Birdsong. Mia believes that not having community is bad for
our health. Former US surgeon general Vivek Murthy said that lone-
liness and weak social connections "are associated with a reduction
in lifespan similar to that caused by smoking fifteen cigarettes a day."
According to Mia, we have bought into an identity that is defined by
personal success, the acquisition of money, and a strong insistence on
self-reliance, and as a result many of us find ourselves lonely, disconnected, and ill-prepared to deal with even the most minor adversity.

She is on the forefront of a new conversation about interdepen-
dence as a basic human need. She proposes a new version of the
American Dream that brings us closer together and allows us to be
vulnerable together—one that has models of success that involve
love, care, and generosity of resource and spirit. In this model, social capital and connectedness make us more resilient.

Take time to deepen your relationships with your genetic or
chosen family to help you weather rapidly changing times.

Here are some ways that you can get beyond linear thinking and develop an exponential mindset:

Move from 10 percent improvement to 10x improvement. The most important thing you can do to move beyond linear thinking is moving beyond making a problem a little less bad to actually fixing the systems that are causing the problem in the first place. For example, imagine you run an afterschool program that serves five hundred elementary school children. You provide reading enrichment programs because students in your district are under-performing in reading. A 10 percent improvement would raise a few more grants and increase your enrollment to 550 students. A 10x improvement would get to the root of the issue and provide all the elementary teachers in the district with enhanced curriculum and coaching support so they were better able to meet students' needs during the day. In this model, you would need fewer staff and financial resources but could reach all five thousand elementary students in the district. This is getting to the transformative scale.

When you start thinking at 10x scale, you need to closely focus on what your ideal future looks like and adjust your strategy, technology, and team to meet that goal.

Learn to weather the deceptive phase of growth. Because we are used to measuring progress linearly, we expect that if we have spent 50 percent of our grant, we should be 50 percent of the way to the goal that we had set. But that is not how exponential growth works, and that confusion creates a huge potential for abandoning an exponential growth model for the issues we care about. The "deceptive growth" point in the chart below is where many people abandon an exponential model and move back to incremental because they are seeing the greatest gap in results. When funders, your team, or the community start to get impatient for results, you have to have patience and perseverance to make it to the point where you start to see the exponential growth that you imagined when you developed your 10x solution.

Help create more realistic success indicators that show slow growth in the first half of your project and rapid growth in the second half.

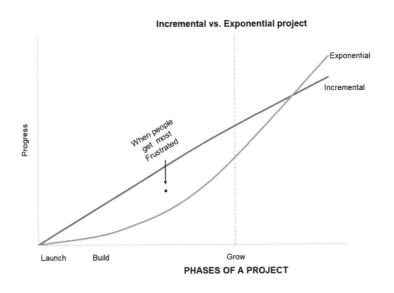

Incremental vs. Exponential project

Build your capacity for rapid change. Traditional command-and-control organizations do not manage the pace of exponential change well. We need to build our capacity to rapidly adapt not just our products or services but our strategies, management practices, and structures. Some organizations have started to make this shift by moving from a strategic plan to strategy screens.

A traditional strategic plan was a five- to ten-year vision that would develop a plan for linear growth using current conditions.

TRISTA HARRIS

61

These types of plans often sat on a bookshelf or were looked at once a year when an organization's CEO was being reviewed. A strategy screen is a much more flexible tool. It gives staff a series of questions that they can ask to guide themselves when making day-to-day decisions.

For example, my former organization, the Minnesota Council on Foundations, underwent a strategic visioning process led by La Piana Consulting. La Piana created a model for real-time strategic planning that is outlined in their book, *The Nonprofit Strategy Revolution*. This helped us figure out our competitive advantage and develop a strategy screen to help staff at all levels in our organization evaluate opportunities on an ongoing basis. These are the criteria in our strategy screen:

Would the proposed activity
1. assist in fulfilling and advancing our purpose?
2. leverage and sustain our competitive advantages, which are our leadership position in the field, deep knowledge of philanthropy, and local relationships?
3. enhance or advance our focus on diversity, equity, inclusion, public policy, or the future of philanthropy?
4. generate the necessary income to cover the full costs of the effort?
5. honor external relationships, engage partners, or foster collaboration?
6. add value to our members by increasing members' impact?
7. lead to greater member engagement with MCF?
8. pose a risk of significantly alienating members and others that we work with?

This allows staff to have a clear direction for their work, and each staff member can make day-to-day decisions in a way that moves in our overall direction. Our decision-making is much more nimble, and we are more able to respond to rapidly changing conditions.

Case Study: Kodak and the Digital Camera

Kodak (founded in 1888) was the world leader in photography. For most of the twentieth century, they dominated the film market; in 1976, Kodak commanded 90 percent of film sales and 85 percent of camera sales in the US. They were such a dominant force in the marketplace that people called memorable life events "Kodak moments."

In 1975 a Kodak employee, Steven Sasson, invented the digital camera. That first camera shot .01 megapixel photos, took twenty-three seconds to record the image to a tape drive, and only shot in black and white. When Steven showed his discovery to executives, they ignored the technology and its implications because they could only see the first square on the chessboard. It would be crazy to think that people would trade in clear, color photos that could be available in just one hour through Fotomats for heavily pixilated, black-and-white photos, so they shelved the technology.

In 1996, Kodak had a $28 billion market capitalization with 95,000 employees. In 2012, Kodak filed for bankruptcy, disrupted by the very technology that they invented and subsequently ignored. In that same year, another company in the digital imagery business, Instagram, was acquired by Facebook for $1 billion. They had just thirteen employees.

There is a long list of companies that have been disrupted by ignoring exponential technologies: video-rental stores by Netflix and other online streaming, record stores by iTunes, traditional taxicabs by Uber, the hotel industry by Airbnb. None of these companies and industries took the time to understand what exponential change meant for their business.

Go Do It!

Here are some ways that you can make sure you aren't blindsided like Kodak:

- **Make time for the future in your present.** I talk to lots of people who say they are too busy to spend time thinking about the future. You have to set aside both the time and mental energy to think about what is possible. Set aside 5 percent of your time or two hours during your workweek to pay attention to the future. I usually set aside Friday afternoons, when my schedule is less hectic, and research trends on issues I care about or watch TED Talks from a variety of fields. This helps me stretch my personal ability to see and understand what is possible.

- **Look backward to appreciate exponential growth.** For the issues that you care about, look way, way back in history to see what kind of progress has been made. If you are working on increased health outcomes for children, what has that progress looked like over the last five hundred years? How has infant mortality decreased? Taking a longer view can show you how extensive the change has already been, which can free you up to think even bigger about what is possible in the future.

- **Don't just focus on better; focus on different.** It is easy to get stuck in a space of incremental improvement. Instead, challenge yourself to imagine what could be different about the issue that you care about. What if it were fully solved?

FutureGood All-Star:

Scott Harrison, founder of charity: water

Deceptive growth also impacts nonprofit organizations. The story of charity: water's deceptive growth is a warning for others that may stop their efforts before they get to exponential growth. The organization was formed in 2006 by Scott Harrison, a former club promoter who was trying to solve the water crisis using specific fundraising asks of his network. Because Scott didn't have a traditional nonprofit background, he approached the challenge of raising money for water wells differently than most organizations.

One of his strategies was encouraging his network to raise money for a well on their birthday using Facebook. He wanted donors to be confident that 100 percent of their donation was building a physical well and not being used for the overhead expenses of the organization. He thought that funding the operation of the nonprofit was a trust barrier for some donors, and he wanted to separate the mission of the organization (building wells) from the infrastructure that was needed to keep charity: water's operation going. While I would love for all donors to understand how important nonprofit infrastructure is to meeting the mission of the organization, I understand that for some donors the trust is not yet there to support that infrastructure. Scott's model was able to eliminate that trust barrier through extreme transparency about which well your money was going to build, and now use live data tracking that shows if your well is still operating and how many gallons of water have been provided.

With this unique fundraising model, charity: water raised $1.7 million in its first full year of operations. By 2017, they had given eight million people around the world access to clean water by funding nearly thirty thousand water projects in twenty-six countries across the world. Over one million people have donated more than $300 million to its cause.

Despite this extreme growth trajectory, in 2008 the organization almost had to shut down its operations. The organization had $800,000 in the bank to build wells but had not raised enough to make payroll. The model of separating the development of wells from the fundraising for the organization's infrastructure was in jeopardy because the growth of infrastructure did not match the pace of the growth of donors for the wells.

The board and the staff had lost faith in the model and encouraged Scott to use the reserves to pay for the organization's overhead cost to fill the gap. He stood with his promise to donors to use their funding exclusively for well development and was ready to shut down the organization. At the last minute, a donor came forward and donated $1 million to cover thirteen months of overhead expenses and helped the organization bridge the gap and help them get to exponential growth.

Today, the operations are funded by 125 families who are part of a program called The Well. The members, who came to Harrison through asks and referrals, donate between $60,000 and $1 million per year for a minimum of three years to exclusively support the overhead expenses of charity: water.

How can you help build a sustainable fundraising base for the cause you care about?

CHAPTER 05:

LOOK AT YOUR MINDSET

"Most successful people begin with two beliefs: the future can be better than the present, and I have the power to make it so."

—David Brooks

On May 21, 1961, President John F. Kennedy asked before a special joint session of Congress for the nation to "commit itself to achieving the goal, before this decade is out, of landing a man on the moon and returning him safely to earth." Going to the moon wasn't just about scientific exploration. After Alan Shepard became the first American in space, Kennedy said, "If we are to win the battle that is now going on around the world between freedom and tyranny, the dramatic achievements in space which occurred in recent weeks should have made clear to us all, as did the Sputnik in 1957, the impact of this adventure on the minds of men everywhere, who are attempting to make a determination of which road they should take." More importantly, Kennedy stressed that taking a "clearly leading role" in space might even "hold the key to our future on earth."

This speech created an urgency to the idea of pursuing a national purpose. Suddenly something that seemed impossible was placed on a timeline, and a whole country stretched to reach the goal. Policymakers found middle ground to fund the ambitious effort, children studied the sciences diligently with the hope that they would someday go to the stars, and new technologies were developed to support the effort, including rockets, life-support systems, lightweight materials, and even pens that could write in zero gravity.

This shared national purpose fueled our country to achieve great scientific achievements, and it changed our mindset about to future.

In 1961, changing the country's mindset was a critically important undertaking. We were in the middle of the Cold War, and space became an extension of this battle, as each side wanted to prove the superiority of its technology, military prowess, and political and economic systems. Announcing the goal of getting a man to the moon and safely back allowed the country to have a tangible guidepost to our role as a global leader.

That mindset is even more critical today than it was when we were in the height of a global conflict. We are living through the greatest era of change since the Industrial Revolution, when we shifted the basic form of production from human muscle to machine, lowered the work week from eighty hours to forty, and freed children from the workforce and moved them to the education system. These changes brought on the growth of cities, changes in family structure, and a global move from sustenance poverty to a growing middle class.

The technological revolution we are currently in is bringing even greater changes. It has greatly expanded access to information that is critical for social, political, and economic engagement. Because the cost of access continues to decline, the digital revolution has democratized access to education and capital around the world.

The digital revolution has also lowered the social costs of relocating anywhere around the globe for economic opportunities. In the past, if you moved to a new city for a job, you weakened your family and social ties. Today, you can stay in constant contact with loved ones from almost anywhere in the world. There are estimates that the next phase of this technological revolution will harness artificial intelligence and robotics to free humans from mentally repetitive work in the same way that the Industrial Revolution freed us from manual work.

These are huge changes, but our brains aren't made to process this type of exponential change that comes with the digital revolution. Our current incremental mindset focuses on making something a little bit better, year after year, while the exponential mindset focuses on making the old thing irrelevant. Steve Cichon has a great piece in the *Huffington Post* about items in a 1991 Radio Shack ad that have become irrelevant because of the iPhone:

- All weather personal stereo, $11.88. I now use my iPhone with an Otter Box.
- AM/FM clock radio, $13.88. iPhone.
- In-Ear Stereo Phones, $7.88. Came with iPhone.
- Microthin calculator, $4.88. Swipe up on iPhone.
- Tandy 1000 TL/3, $1599. I actually owned a Tandy 1000, and I used it for games and word processing. I now do most of both of those things on my phone.
- VHS Camcorder, $799. iPhone.
- Mobile Cellular Telephone, $199. Obvs.
- Mobile CB, $49.95. Ad says "You'll never drive 'alone' again!" iPhone.
- 20-Memory Speed-Dial phone, $29.95.
- Deluxe Portable CD Player, $159.95. 80 minutes of music, or 80 hours of music? iPhone.

- 10-Channel Desktop Scanner, $99.55. I still have a scanner, but I have a scanner app, too. iPhone.
- Easiest-to-Use Phone Answerer, $49.95. iPhone voicemail.
- Handheld Cassette Tape Recorder, $29.95. I use the Voice Memo app almost daily.

He calculates that it would have cost $3,054.82 in 1991 to buy all the stuff in this ad that you can now do with your phone. That amount is roughly equivalent to about $5,484.41 in 2017 dollars.

The iPhone wasn't about incrementally improving the existing phone; it was creating an exponential shift in how we communicate and interact with the world.

Futurist and inventor Ray Kurzweil describes accelerating returns to scale as an innovation in the system creating the conditions where even the rate of change grows exponentially because each part of the growth curve is benefiting from the last period of growth. In his 2001 essay on the Law of Accelerating Returns, he says, "An analysis of the history of technology shows that technological change is exponential, contrary to the common-sense 'intuitive linear' view. So we won't experience 100 years of progress in the 21st century — it will be more like 20,000 years of progress (at today's rate). The 'returns,' such as chip speed and cost-effectiveness, also increase exponentially. There's even exponential growth in the rate of exponential growth."

We must change our mindsets to allow us to move past the current mental limitations that inhibit us from dealing more effectively with the sheer pace and explosive magnitude of exponential growth. This is the only way that we will benefit from the possibilities of the future. This is a hard shift to make because we have to move from a mindset that is predictable to one in which we need the courage and patience to build a foundation for growth, even when the results aren't yet apparent. We have to unlearn familiar ways of thinking and embrace the unknown. Here's how to do that:

Become Persistently Adaptable

According to Charles Darwin, it is not the most intelligent or strongest species that survives; rather, it is the one best able to adapt. However, humans have a love-hate relationship with change. We happily embrace change when it brings us new innovations that make our lives easier, but if we are the ones that have to do the changing, we resist it. John Kobara, executive vice president and chief operating officer of the California Community Foundation, says, "We want stability, but what we need is persistent adaptability."

The reason that humans crave stability has to do with the way that our brains process new information. In Laurence Gonzales's book *Everyday Survival: Why Smart People Do Stupid Things*, he talks about the stupid mistakes we make when we work from a mental script that does not match the requirements of real-world situations.

One of the reasons this happens is the way that the brain processes new information. It creates what Gonzales calls "behavioral scripts," or mental models that automate almost every action we take. For example, we have built a behavioral script for how to eat soup or what to do if an angry dog is running toward us. These mental models make our world more simple, so we don't have to deeply think about every decision that we make, especially if we have to make that decision quickly. They influence not only our actions but also what we pay attention to and believe. Gonzales says, "We tend not to notice things that are inconsistent with the models, and we tend not to try what the scripts tells us is bad or impossible."

The efficiency that we gain with these behavioral scripts comes with a significant downside: they can take our attention away from important information coming to us from our environment. The behavioral scripts encourage us to dismiss signals because the message we get from our scripts is that we already know about it. So we make decisions about a situation that, as Gonzales puts it, "aren't really decisions in the real sense of the word. They're simply automated behaviors." Mental scripts also create the "this is how we have always done it" problem. We tend to generalize into the future what worked in the past and avoid anything that failed.

During times of exponential change, it is extremely dangerous and shortsighted to rely on mental models for decision making; instead we need to follow John Kobara's advice and develop our skills in persistent adaptability.

Persistent comes from the Latin verb *persistere*, which means "to continue with strength." Adaptability is your ability to change given changing circumstances. Persistent adaptability is your aptitude at consistently using change as an opportunity for growth.

Persistent adaptability is not just about being flexible when change comes; it is about anticipating that change and using it as a growth opportunity. Those who don't embrace change with adaptability usually get blindsided by it. Persistent adaptability allows you to respond to new conditions rather than reacting using existing mental models.

So how do you develop this skill?

Notice when you are using existing behavioral scripts. Making time to be reflective about your leadership can help you identify when you are using existing scripts. Here are some questions to consider:

- Does the same type of problem come up over and over in your organization or in your life? What is it?

- How do you usually approach these repeating problems?
- How successful is your current strategy at solving that problem?
- What blocks currently exist in solving that problem?
- Is there a new behavior or way of viewing the problem that would help you overcome those blocks?

When you notice the same type of problem coming up over and over again, it may mean that the behavioral script that you are using in no longer effective. Determine new approaches to help you get out of the zone of automatic responses.

Ask new questions. Instead of asking how you can mitigate a problem, ask how you can make the problem no longer exist. Our natural instinct is to ask narrow questions to get us to a quick, but narrow, solution. This is not helpful when you are looking for new possibilities in a complex system.

New questions could include:
- What would a ridiculous solution look like? Why is it ridiculous?
- What are my possible blind spots on this issue?
- What is most surprising to me in this situation?
- What solution would be the opposite of what I'd normally do?
- Who is most impacted by this problem?
- Who is the core beneficiary of this problem?
- When did this problem really begin?
- When did this problem get worse?
- Where does this problem show up the most?
- Where does this problem not exist?

Different questions can help build a more flexible, agile mindset and can help you embrace challenges as new opportunities.

Create the Breathing Room to Creatively Solve Problems

Our brains are constantly being stimulated, which makes it difficult to stand back and anticipate what is coming next. As we start to go down the rabbit hole of understanding exponential change, we can get overwhelmed by the implications and become paralyzed by the options. We have to purposefully change how we interact with information and how we are accessing that information.

So, how do you create breathing room?

Learn to meditate. You are probably thinking that you didn't start reading a book about the future to get advice on how to breathe more thoughtfully. But the research on mindfulness suggests that meditation builds skills like attention, memory, and even emotional intelligence. It also reduces stress and anxiety, boosting your ability to perform under stress and stay resilient. Meditation can develop the foundation of a flexible and agile mindset that is the core of thinking exponentially. Meditation creates space to think. A few minutes in the morning and again in the evening are all that is necessary to help center yourself and regain your focus.

Gaiam has a wonderful step-by-step guide on how to start meditating:

1. Sit or lie comfortably.
2. Close your eyes.
3. Make no effort to control the breath; simply breathe naturally.
4. Focus your attention on the breath and on how the body moves with each inhalation and exhalation. Notice the movement of your body as you breathe. Observe your chest, shoulders, rib cage, and belly. Simply focus your attention on your breath

without controlling its pace or intensity. If your mind wanders, return your focus back to your breath.

Try this activity for ten minutes in the morning and ten minutes at night. I have also really enjoyed guided meditations; there are many available on YouTube. If you are more of a data geek, the Muse meditation headset measures your brainwaves during meditation to help you keep track of your progress.

Meditation strengthens your brain in the same way that exercise strengthens your body. Doing meditation consistently will help you change your mindset.

Take breaks from technology. As we covered in the last chapter, technology can become a constant distraction rather than a tool. Determine when and how you will use technology and don't fall into the trap of cellphone notifications telling you when to interact with technology. Setting times twice a day that you will check email, rather than having a notification that sounds each time you get a new message, will let you decide when and how you will engage. Setting a timer when you are surfing the internet will help you avoid spending hours browsing Facebook when you meant to spend fifteen minutes there.

Sometimes we just need to step away from technology completely to regroup. Reboot has started a project called the Sabbath Manifesto, which carves out one day a week for you to unwind, unplug, relax, reflect, get outdoors, and get with loved ones by eliminating technology use on that day. They even have a cellphone sleeping bag for you to put away your cellphone during your sabbath.

Technology is a powerful tool, but constant use can shorten our attention span and disrupt our sleep. Set aside time to step away.

Limit the bad news. Peter Diamonds of the X Prize Foundation famously encourages people to stop watching the news. He states that our brains "pay 10 times more attention to negative news (an evolutionary attribute that kept us alive thousands of years ago). Today the news media abuses this . . . they are a drug pusher and negative news is their drug. Choose how and where you get your news feed. Proactively seek it out instead of being fed every murder, in HD, over and over again. Let the data do the talking, and allow yourself to opt for abundance."

After a string of terrible events in 2014, President Obama said, "The world has always been messy. In part, we're just noticing now because of social media and our capacity to see in intimate detail the hardships that people are going through." We are seeing these tragedies in greater detail and for longer than we have in the past. A 2013 study found that people that were present at the site of the Boston Marathon bombing or were a part of the Boston-area lockdown had less acute stress than people who watched six or more hours of bombing-related media exposure daily in the weeks after the bombing. We are reenacting trauma for hours a day through social media and news intake, and that is hurting us even more than being directly affected by a trauma.

Luckily, we have a choice about how much of this trauma we are exposed to. I've started blocking news websites that I check compulsively, and when there is a significant, depressing news event, I will often disconnect from media altogether to ensure that I don't have to be retraumatized from watching the news replays. Find ways to limit your consumption of bad news.

Be willing to take risks. Human beings are a pretty risk-averse species. I'm guessing that when our brains were being wired, it was more important that we didn't get eaten by a lion than if we had an inert craving to try new things. But being willing to take risks is critical for a few reasons:

- You open up the edges of possibility. T.S. Eliot said, "Only those who will risk going too far can possibly find out how far it is possible to go." When you take a risk, you reopen yourself previously unseen opportunities and rewards. It is only by trying a new path that new rewards are possible.

- There is less competition. Most people are playing it safe. When you start to take risks, especially on issues that you are passionate about, you are in the space of innovation and new possibilities.

- Failure gives you new skill sets. Even if an opportunity doesn't pan out, it can teach you new skills and stretch you in new ways.

It has been really helpful for me to think, "What is the worst thing that can happen?" when I am avoiding taking a risk. For example, if I were thinking about giving a speech in front of a large audience and worried about it, I could go through all of the terrible scenarios. Maybe I will forget what I have to say, or I'll get nervous and repeat myself, or I'll fall. This helps me get into solution mode to manage the risk. I could practice the speech a few times so I'm less nervous. I could wear low heels and check the stage for any cords before I get up there to make that result less likely to happen. If the worst actually does happen, it probably it won't be that big of a deal for the audience, or I will seem more human and approachable.

Case Study: Weekly Review Process

Examining your mindset is tricky because it lives in your blind spots, but a way that I've found to examine it is a weekly review process. Every Friday, I ask myself a series of questions that I keep in a single Word document. I learned the technique from Laura Garnett, a performance strategist. The purpose of these questions is to reveal what's responsible for the high points and low points of your work week. When you are able to see the underlying root causes of how you feel about your week, you can begin to make changes to your activities and mindset so that the next week will feel different. This leads to changes in how you see the world, and it is a reminder that you are responsible for the success of your work and personal life. Garnett suggests the following questions:

1. What was the most enjoyable work activity of the week?
2. How many enjoyable work moments did you have?
3. How many frustrating or boring moments did you have?
4. How would you describe your impact on others you work with, your customers, or those whom you came into contact with this week?
5. Is this the type of impact you want?
6. If not, what prompted this change in desired impact?
7. Were you challenged this week?
8. Were you bored?
9. What were your biggest and most exciting challenges this past week?
10. How confident did you feel this week?
11. Did you have any negative mental chatter about yourself?
12. Are you practicing actively believing that you can achieve whatever it is you have set your sights on?
13. Are you committed to having joy and groundbreaking results at work?
14. What distractions came up this week that prevented you from getting the most out of your job?
15. How can you avoid that going forward?

The future is not just this external force. For you, the most important aspect of the future is what sort of person you will be and what your life will look like. Through my weekly review process, I watch for trends in how I'm growing as a leader and as a person. I do this every Friday morning, and it takes me about twenty minutes. It has been my greatest tool for noticing blind spots in my mindset.

I write my answers down in a single Word document that has new entries for each week. This activity serves a few purposes. It allows me to journal in a focused way, with a consistent set of questions. I start to notice patterns in how I respond to hard situations, and in the future I can use that knowledge to make a new decision. For example, if I have a project fail or a relationship becomes suddenly difficult, I look back to previous weeks and months to see if I can tell where it started to go wrong. Often it shows up as less excitement for a specific project or small concerns about a relationship. Those signs, if ignored, can become bigger issues.

It is hard work to consistently look at yourself with an eye toward what can be improved, but you can only be a more effective leader if you do that hard work.

Adding time for a weekly review on your schedule will help you see blind spots and notice positive and negative patterns over time.

FutureGood All-Star:

Nicholas Haan, vice president of impact at Singularity University

Nicholas Haan has worked at the intersection of science, technology, social challenges, and innovation for the last twenty-five years. His issues of focus have included disaster relief, food security, environment, energy, public health, education, genetics, and information systems. And his affiliations have included the United Nations, governments, universities, donor agencies, and nongovernmental organizations.

Nick is currently vice president of impact and on the faculty at Singularity University. SU is a think tank designed to educate, inspire, and empower leaders to apply exponential technologies to address humanity's grand challenges, and Nick sits at the center of that work. What impresses me most about Nick is that he's not afraid to work on the world's toughest problems, but he wants to harness the power of exponential technology to have an impact on the issues.

Nicolas has developed a mindset that allows him to consistently view the world as it might look in five to ten years. This allows him to think about how the tools that Singularity University is working on—nanotechnology, robotics, blockchain—can be used to address humanity's greatest challenges. He has done this by surrounding himself with big thinkers and translating their ideas for people that do good for a living.

Who are the big thinkers that you can spend time with to expand your view of what is possible?

Go Do It!

Here are some ways to adjust your mindset:

- **Give yourself space**. Take some time away from technology on a consistent basis to daydream and allow your brain to make new connections between ideas. Your ability to understand what is coming next is a balance between taking in new information and ideas and giving those ideas the space and time to grow.
- **Adapt.** Examine your regular behaviors and ways of approaching problems by using the weekly review process. Which of your behavioral scripts need to be revised for changing conditions?
- **Take risks.** Practice taking small risks so that you are more comfortable when it is time to take big risks. Ask for a discount at a coffee shop, say hello to a stranger, raise your hand to take on a hard assignment. Constantly stretching your ability to take risks will help you expand your mindset.

CHAPTER 06:

LOOK: TODAY IS GIVING YOU CLUES ABOUT TOMORROW

"The world is full of obvious things which nobody by any chance ever observes."

—Sherlock Holmes

I understand that it is easy to become overwhelmed when you are thinking about the future. The possibilities feel endless, and it is hard enough to stay on top of what is happening today, let alone predict what will happen tomorrow. There is an even more insidious version of this line of thinking: it may feel irresponsible to be concerned about the future when we are facing problems today. I experienced this when I was co-leading the African American Leadership Forum. When we talked about a fifty-year vision for our community that would benefit our children and grandchildren, there was inevitably someone who would push back and ask us how we could possibly think that we had the luxury to care about the next fifty years when children were dying in the streets today.

As a social sector and as people that care about societal issues, we need to break free from this zero-sum thinking. We have the time and capacity to work on the problems of today, and we have a responsibility to create solutions for the future. Understanding what is coming next is critical to disentangling today's problems.

This chapter will give you the tools to notice the signals of the future that exist today and help you learn to keep track of those signals. Your responsibility as a future-focused leader is taking facts about the present and your hunches about the future and turning all of that into a clear action plan for your organization moving forward.

Here are some tools to help you identify signals of the future:

Find new sources of information. It is human nature to spend time with people who think like we do. If we work in education, we spend our days in schools with other educators, we go to education conferences, we read education blogs, and many of our friends share our profession. We spend time around people who probably share the same set of solutions and viewpoints. This makes it incredibly difficult to find new solutions. You've got to look outside of your regular box.

My favorite place to look for new ideas from other viewpoints is TED Talks. TED was created in 1984 after cofounder Richard Saul Wurman observed a powerful convergence of three fields: technology, entertainment, and design. The first TED conference included a demonstration of the compact disc, the ebook, and cutting-edge 3D graphics from Lucasfilm.

In 2001, Chris Anderson became the curator of TED and used his media experience to bring it to a worldwide audience through free online access to TED Talks. TED gives a platform to the most interesting people on Earth and lets them communicate their passion.

Because TED speakers come from many, many disciplines and countries, it is a cornucopia of new ideas. I've found the best ideas by watching random TED Talks and thinking about how the speaker's topic ties to the work that I am doing. For example, as my organization was developing our calendar of programs for the next year, I was trying to think about how to engage more of our membership in our programs. I randomly selected Susan Cain's talk, "The Power of Introverts." While watching that talk, I had a revelation that our programming was all built for extroverts. You needed to come to our programs and network with your peers, and the best way to dig deeper into the speaker's content was to raise your hand and ask a question. An even better way to make a positive impression with your peers was to be the presenter for our peer learning sessions. All of this sounds miserable and exhausting for introverts, who might lose their energy when they have to interact in that way.

This clarity was the driving force for the development of our online peer networking platform called the Hub. The Hub is a place for our membership to post questions and resources online in a member-only online environment. People can engage and connect with peers who have similar jobs or are funding in similar areas. New members are becoming our most important connectors and information curators on this platform because they are able to engage in a way that plays to their strengths.

Using networks to identify signals of the future. It is really hard to identify signals of the future in a vacuum. You need to talk with people and explore what new signals might mean. I do this by scheduling coffees or lunches with interesting people in my network that I don't get to spend a lot of time with, or with new people who I'd like to be a part of my network. It is critical to build a large and varied network to have as many nodes as possible giving you new perspectives on the problems that you are working on. If you spend all of your time with people in your sector or geographic area who approach problems similarly, you won't be exposed to new ideas and ways of thinking.

While it is really easy to get in my comfort zone with my current network or in my current field, some of my best ideas have come from when I spent time in uncomfortable places, where I felt like an outsider.

I'll share a very frustrating experience I had when I tried to network outside of my comfort zone. When I was first learning about futurism, I decided to attend the World Futurism Society Conference. During the conference, I found myself getting crabby and withdrawn. Usually I really enjoy conferences, and I couldn't understand why this one was so different. I even tried to find a flight that returned sooner so I could get out of there. It finally dawned on me when I was listening to one of the keynote speakers make fun of a former leader of the World Future Society. I realized I was crabby because I wasn't in on the joke. I didn't know the people, the buzzwords, and the inside jokes. I was the newbie.

I was used to being in spaces where I was always comfortable and fully understood the context of the space. I knew the speakers at the conferences I attended, or I was the speaker and I was the one making the corny inside joke from the stage. My frustration was not that I was an outsider but that I had to learn and grow, and I wasn't used to that feeling. I had been a fully developed professional in my field for so long that I didn't remember what it felt like to be new. Going back to a learner's mindset can be difficult, but it was necessary to take my skills to the next level.

After I understood that this feeling was growing and not just frustration, I stayed and developed new relationships.

Spend some time learning about other worlds. Societies often have set types of solutions to problems. If you are stuck, find out how other places solve the problem. Would looking at the early childhood system in Sweden give you lessons in St. Louis? Would looking at how birds migrate give you ideas on how to manage traffic on highways? Would looking at a deep-sea ecosystem and the relationship between sharks and algae help you start to understand how your local nonprofit ecosystem operates?

Let's say you have been tasked with developing recommendations for a citywide transportation plan. You can find new ways of approaching the issue by googling things like:

- most efficient international transportation system
- wildebeest great migration
- communication during starling murmuration
- Norway bicycle highway
- world's most unusual models of transportation
- Kenya's Matatu van system

You probably won't find cut-and-paste recommendations, but you will stretch your thinking about what is possible.

Develop a system for tracking trends. The next step is to keep track of all of the things that you are learning. Evernote works well for me as a place to store interesting ideas and trends that I am noticing. I have notebooks for topics that I am watching (future of philanthropy, self-driving cars, alternative currency, future of education and work), and I have also set up Google alerts for those topics. I keep links or notes from things that I am surprised about or that match trends I am anticipating about that topic. In addition to saving these notes on Evernote, I often share the trends I'm seeing on Twitter (@TristaHarris) to get feedback.

Here is an example of an article that caught my eye and a note that I added for myself to notice the trend.

Elon Musk unveils new solar roof tiles, Japan Times

Elon Musk showcased his ambitions to make Tesla Motors Inc. a clean-energy behemoth on Friday, unveiling a new solar roof product at Universal Studios in Los Angeles.

As the sun set, Musk told hundreds of guests gathered in an outside courtyard on the *Desperate Housewives* set that Tesla and SolarCity Corp., the company that he chairs and which he aims to acquire, will make solar roofs that look better than normal roofs. He then showcased several houses with solar tiles gracefully embedded. Because the tiles are fully integrated into the roofs, many guests in attendance could not tell that they were solar.

"How do we have a solar roof that is better than a normal roof, looks better, last longer?" said Musk. "You want to pull your neighbors over and say, 'Check out this sweet roof.'"

The larger idea is that homeowners will generate electricity for their home with solar power, then store that electricity in a home battery known as a Powerwall. You can fill up your battery during the day, then discharge it at night when the sun sets. The latest iteration, Powerwall 2, weighs 269 pounds (122 kg) and is designed to be floor- or wall-mounted inside or outside.

My notes:

The cost is less than a traditional roof and it looks like there is a mechanism for storing power. This seems to solve 2 big problems (cost of solar power for homes and storage of that power). I wonder how the installation capabilities will get built up?

Also interesting that Musk unveiled the roof at a dramatic set that felt like a neighborhood. Think more about how the unveiling of new ideas helps build credibility.

Follow up:

☐ *Is Summit Academy, our local construction training program for hard-to-employ people, training their students how to install these roofs? This could be a good growth skill for their students. Ask their training director.*

☐ *Is a Habitat for Humanity partnership is possible? Could this technology keep ongoing utility costs lower for low-income home-owners? Ask their board member Irene at our next Women's Economic Roundtable lunch.*

Here's another example:

> **Finland has created a digital money system for refugees, World Economic Forum**
>
> Between January 2014 and June 2017, the Finnish immigration authority received 41,241 asylum applications, mostly from citizens of Iraq, Afghanistan, Syria, Somalia, and Eritrea. For those granted asylum, key challenges remained. Without identification papers, they faced a long wait to get work permits or bank accounts. And without access to financial services, they couldn't bank their wages, pay bills, or start to recover their identities.
>
> So one Finnish start-up came up with a solution. Debit cards without a bank. MONI has developed a prepaid debit card that circumvents the need for a bank account or identity papers. The card is linked to a unique digital identity stored on a blockchain—the same technology that underpins Bitcoin and other digital currencies.
>
> Two years ago, MONI partnered with the Finnish government to provide refugees with their monthly allowance, which until then had been paid in cash.

My notes:

Other communities that are unbanked might benefit from this solution. The blockchain aspect would eliminate fraud worries.

Follow up:

☐ *Share MONI contact information with Catholic Charities' Homeless Outreach program.*

☐ *Would a blockchain solution system be an improvement for Minnesota's refugee resettlement program?*

Some people prefer physical notebooks or notecards to keep track of similar trends. Use what works best for you, but keep all the notes in the same electronic or physical location because it is hard to notice trends if you have information scattered over too many locations.

Case Study: 831 Dinners to Harvest Trends

A few years ago I was introduced to the idea of a Jeffersonian dinner. When Thomas Jefferson was developing the idea of an American democracy, he invited people with different backgrounds and perspectives to share a meal and debate the future of the country.

I've created a version of the Jeffersonian model called 831 dinners. It consists of eight people, sitting together for three hours over dinner, having one transformational conversation about an issue of critical importance. After the Charleston Church shooting, I decided that I would host a dinner on the future of race relations in America. I have also hosted dinners on topics like civic disaster preparation and the future of philanthropy. A few things I have learned after hosting a number of these dinners:

- **A curated guest list is critical.** Developing a guest list that gives you a diversity of backgrounds and experiences makes for a richer conversation. I aim for a balance of men and women, racial diversity, and people with a variety of professional experiences that relate to and are completely separate from the topic at hand. I have found that artists and organizers provide an interesting conversational balance to academics and foundation leaders. You don't have to know everyone at the table well; it is a great opportunity to deepen relationships. Don't invite people who won't listen. This is a conversation, not just an opportunity for one person to pontificate.

- **Make sure that guests have background on each other.** For each dinner, I share a bio of each participant and a photo. It allows the guests to have a little bit of context before they are at the table, and they are less likely to cancel if they feel like they are part of a group.

- **Food and wine make everything better.** For each meal, I make sure that I understand dietary needs and provide a family-style dinner. There are flowers and candles so that it feels like a dinner amongst friends and not a focus group. I pick foods that aren't too messy to eat and keep a bottle of wine on the table as well as a variety of nonalcoholic drinks.

- **Start with the personal.** We start with introductions around the table; each guest answers the starting question that places them in the conversation as a human being, not as a representative from a specific organization. An example is, "When was the first time you felt hopeful about race relations in the United States?"

- **The host is a guide.** The job of the host is to make everyone comfortable and move the conversation along. You also need to make sure that one person isn't dominating the conversation and that quiet voices get heard.

- **Close with a commitment.** Give participants an opportunity at the end of the conversation to talk about what they have learned or appreciated from the conversation and what they will do next as a result.

An initially unintended benefit of the dinners was that they also helped me identify trends across fields. I record each of the dinners and then have them transcribed. Looking through those notes across multiple dinners, I noticed similarities: growing disconnection between communities, individuals across sectors that have a burning desire to make the world a better place and are doing it through their work, and concerns about how changes in technology will change who we are as humans.

Go Do It!

Here are some ways to see the clues that today is giving you about tomorrow:

Find a new network. What are three new networks or associations you can start to spend time with? Attend one of their networking programs or happy hours to see if it adds value, and be willing to work through the discomfort of being in a new space. A note to introverts: This step may feel like a challenge, but building networks is critical to broadening your perspective. Find a small networking event to start.

Set up a Google alert.
1. Go to google.com/alerts in your browser.
2. Enter a search term for the topic you want to track. Try "future of (issue you care about)."
3. Choose *Show Options* to narrow the alert to a specific source, language, and/or region.
4. Select *Create Alert*.
   This will expose you to new ideas about the topic you care about. If you find a blog or website that consistently provides information

on the topic you are interested in, subscribe to their updates so you have sources of information for your two hours a week of time focused on the future.

Create your future trends notebook. Pick the place that you will keep track of trends in a physical or electronic notebook and schedule your weekly time to pay attention to future trends.

Futuregood All-Star:

Amy Webb, founder of Future Today Institute

Amy Webb is a quantitative futurist. She is a professor of strategic foresight at NYU Stern School of Business and the founder of the Future Today Institute, a foresight and strategy firm that helps organizations and their leaders prepare for complex futures. In her book *The Signals Are Talking*, Webb helps readers learn to spot emerging trends. She believes that there is not one predetermined future but many possible futures that each depend on a variety of choices that we make today.

Here is Webb's forecasting methodology:
- **Step 1: The fringe.** Make observations and harness information from the fringes of society or a particular research area.
- **Step 2: Uncover hidden patterns.** Categorize information from the fringe into patterns: contradictions, inflections, practices, hacks, extremes, and rarities.
- **Step 3: Ask the right questions.** Stop and ask the right questions to determine whether a pattern is really a trend.
- **Step 4: Calculate the ETA** Where is the trend in its trajectory? Will it continue to take shape over time? Is the timing right for your organization?
- **Step 5: Write scenarios:** Scenarios inform the strategy you will create to take necessary action on the trend.
- **Step 6: Pressure-test the action:** Are the scenarios comprehensive enough? Is the strategy that you are taking the right one for the future?

If you are looking for strategies to make your predictions about the future more sophisticated, Amy's books are a great place to start.

What can you start uncovering the hidden patterns that exist in the issues that you care about?

CHAPTER 07:

LOOK: SCENARIO PLANNING FOR DO-GOODERS

"A spider is wise because it hunts before its prey arrives."
—Unknown

Scenario planning is a structured way for organizations to think about the future. Scenarios are just stories about how the future might unfold and how those future conditions could impact the organization.

Scenarios challenge your conventional assumptions and help you deal with times of uncertainty. Since they are written about the high-level forces for change, they remain a relevant planning tool for many years, and they can be customized for many different uses.

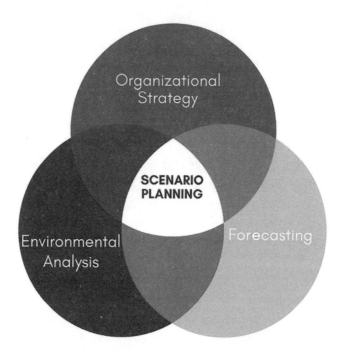

Scenario planning is the intersection of organizational strategy, which is the sum of the actions the organization plans to undertake to meet its long-term goals; forecasting, which is using data from the past to estimate future trends; and environmental analysis, which asks that you understand the factors external to the organization that can impact its operations.

Scenario planning is a critical skill for do-gooders. It allows you to identify a variety of possible futures, and then you can use the best- and worst-case scenarios as planning tools. This is a tangible way to start thinking about how the signals of the future that you identified in the last chapter could play out in your organization or for the issues that you care about. As new opportunities arise, having many possible ways that you think about the future is better than just having a strategic plan.

During times of significant change (e.g., now), people can get paralyzed with uncertainty. Having already conceived of possible scenarios gives you a small number of plans to move forward with and can help you narrow when to act. Here's a very simple example: Let's say you develop two possible scenarios for your organization's plan concerning a big government grant. The first scenario could lay out the strategy if you receive the grant, and the second scenario could lay out what happens if you don't receive the grant. Then you have a clear path moving forward regardless of the grant outcome.

Scenarios are often used by the military, government agencies, and large businesses to create new strategies, stress-test existing strategies, and create a culture of strategic thinking in organizations.

Scenarios are developed for the many outside forces that impact the organization. So if you were a nonprofit that provided food to people in South Sudan, you might develop management scenarios about refugees and global conflict. These scenario stories wouldn't explicitly talk about hunger in South Sudan, but they would involve conditions that your organization may have to respond to. The scenarios allow you to test current or proposed strategies against hypothetical scenarios.

PAX, a Netherlands peace foundation, laid out scenarios for South Sudan in 2020. They present five scenarios for the future of South Sudan:

1. **United in diversity:** The 2015 peace agreement holds and the peace process leads to a further decentralized federal system and better guarantees for good governance. The organization of free and fair elections is one of the first steps in a long and difficult process toward sustainable peace.

2. **Divided leadership:** After the opposition rejects the election results, its forces occupy part of the country, effectively splitting the country in two. The war stabilizes along a front line, and consequently some of the improvements that had been made in good governance and development are maintained.

3. **Fragmentation:** After the peace agreement breaks down, slowly the government collapses and opposition groups fragment. South Sudan lacks any form of national governance system. Politics is local and about the highest price: life and security.

4. **21 Kingdoms:** After a bloody victory of the Sudan People's Liberation Movement in Opposition (SPLM-IO), South Sudan is divided into twenty-one states based on ethnic power divisions. Some states do reasonably well, while others face ethnic conflicts and autocracy.

5. **Dictatorship:** With the SPLM-IO reduced to a low-level insurgency, the Sudan People's Liberation Movement in Government (SPLM-IG) embraces anyone willing to return back to the party. The new twenty-eight states do not lead to further decentralization as the SPLM-IG leadership reduces the political space for any remaining opposition and dissent.

The food nonprofit servicing South Sudan should examine these scenarios and ask themselves the following questions:
- What are the opportunities for our organization to meet the needs of more South Sudanese citizens in each of these scenarios?
- What are the unique challenges in each of these scenarios?

- Are there strategies that are effective in multiple scenarios
  or in all scenarios?

Investing organizational time and energy in understanding
what each of these scenarios means for their work will ensure that
they develop strategies that work in multiple scenarios and can develop plans of action for each of the scenarios in case they become
a reality.

Scenarios Cheat Code

Later in this chapter, I will describe a few simple ways to get started
in creating your own scenarios, but first I'd like to give you some
advice. If you are just getting started with scenario planning, start
by using someone else's scenarios, like the previous South Sudan
example. There are tons of businesses, government agencies, and
nonprofit organizations that are partnering with professional futurists to develop well-researched scenarios, many of which could
be useful as you think about your organization's future or the future of the issue that you care about. Save yourself some time and
trouble by using existing resources first.

A few sources for scenarios:

- **Shell Scenarios:** Since the 1970s, Shell has been developing possible visions of the future to help their company's leadership explore ways forward and make better decisions. Shell describes
  their scenarios as "plausible and challenging descriptions of
  the future landscape. They stretch our thinking and help us to
  make crucial choices in times of uncertainty and transitions
  as we grapple with tough energy and environmental issues."
  They have an expert team that is constantly developing and
  refining scenarios that have global significance and have made

these scenarios public so that other organizations can utilize them for their planning. Recent scenarios covered six possible types of future cities, looked into meeting energy needs while reducing carbon emission to net zero, and imagined a world where the status quo of power and influence remains the same and an alternative vision where power and influence have devolved. Search for Shell Scenarios online as a tool for your organization to react to.

- **RAND Corporation:** RAND is a nonprofit global policy think tank that was created in 1948 to offer research and analysis to the United States armed forces. They have a deep base of research and scenarios and have expertise on issues like child policy, civil and criminal justice, education, health, international policy, labor markets, national security, infrastructure, energy, environment, corporate governance, economic development, intelligence policy, crisis management and disaster preparation, population and regional studies, science and technology, social welfare, terrorism, arts policy, and transportation. They offer a variety of scenarios that can be helpful as you are looking at community conditions and possible upcoming trends.

- **Good old Google search:** Searching for phrases like *scenarios for schools of tomorrow, future cities, future of healthcare, future of global conflict, technology change,* or *future of family structure* can introduce you to a whole new group of organizations that have developed scenarios that will be useful for your organization or issue area.

Other Scenario Planning Tools:

Preferred-future visioning. This is a useful tool if you want to use scenarios to help people see what the future could look like if they worked together toward a common goal. Think of this as a cross between a scenario and a vision statement. However, instead of the internal organizational goals in a vision statement, the preferred-future narrative describes how you would like conditions external to the organization to change. It provides a target list of activities for manipulating the organization's operating environment.

First, determine the right people to be a part of your planning process. A mix of senior leadership, board members, line staff, and community members that are impacted by the organization is a strong combination to craft a thoughtful future vision. Then make sure that all participants understand that this process is about describing the ideal future that you are building toward *outside* of your organization.

There are a few ways to develop a preferred vision, but I recommend using a design thinking process with broad community and stakeholder input. This will help you set aside your own assumptions about what the end result should look like.

Stanford's Hasso-Plattner Institute of Design (d. school) has developed a five-step model that is useful for developing your preferred vision.

To craft your preferred future, follow these steps:

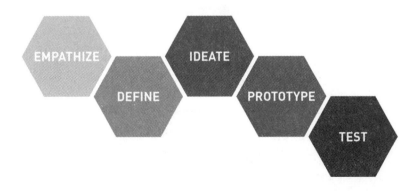

1. Empathize

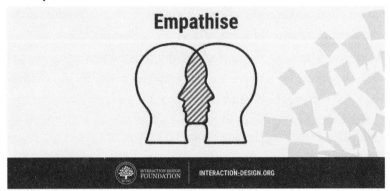

Author/Copyright holder: Teo Yu Siang and Interaction DesignFoundation
(www.interaction-design.org). Copyright license: CC BY-NC-SA 3.0

The first stage is to gain an empathetic understanding of the environment you are trying to create. This involves consulting experts and community members to understand what the ideal future could look like from each of their perspectives. Empathy is critical to the design process and allows the people involved to set aside their own assumptions to gain insight into the needs of community members.

2. Define

Author/Copyright holder: Teo Yu Siang and Interaction DesignFoundation
(www.interaction-design.org). Copyright license: CC BY-NC-SA 3.0

In this stage, you put together the information that you have gathered during the first stage and define the conditions. Analyze your observations and synthesize them in order to define the core opportunities you and your team have identified up to this point.

3. Ideate

Author/Copyright holder: Teo Yu Siang and Interaction DesignFoundation (www.interaction-design.org). Copyright license: CC BY-NC-SA 3.0

During this stage, you start generating ideas about how to make the opportunities from the previous stage come to life. Having a brainstorming session where great and terrible ideas are all captured can help you start to look at alternative ways to create those ideal conditions.

4. Prototype

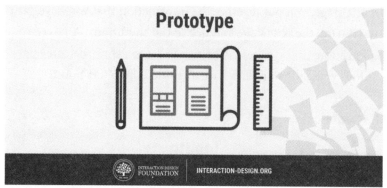

The planning team will develop a number of preferred futures that are either visuals or very short paragraphs. These preferred futures describe the operating environment that the organization would work in and the steps needed to actually achieve it. For example:

Our community has clean air, water, and soil for now and for future generations.

Steps needed:
- *Clear environmental protections for local community.*
- *An economy that is built on environmentally responsible methods.*
- *Community members that provide political cover and personal choices that enhance our natural environment.*

These prototype preferred futures can be shared and tested with the full planning team, people in the organization, and a small number of community members. The aim of this step is to find the most compelling preferred futures.

5. Test

Author/Copyright holder: Teo Yu Siang and Interaction DesignFoundation
(www.interaction-design.org). Copyright license: CC BY-NC-SA 3.0

The planners continue to test the preferred futures that were de-veloped in the prototype phase. Because this is an iterative model, these futures can continue to be refined and altered based on con-tinued feedback.

This preferred-future document can be a powerful communica-tions tool that helps people understand what their aligned work can lead to. It helps staff and partners stay motivated during challeng-ing times and can be a powerful fundraising tool.

After the plan is complete, it should be shared widely with stake-holders so they can see their part in moving forward this preferred future.

Oxford Scenarios Planning Model

Researchers at the University of Oxford have developed a unique scenario-planning method that helps leaders realize their role in using scenarios in planning to enable their organizations to learn faster and better about changing conditions. I think this model is especially useful now as we enter a time of a rapidly increasing pace of change. This model helps you find ways to create your future, identify new challenges, and avoid missing unprecedented opportunities.

Step 1: Determine which driving forces won't change in your scenario. For example:

- Federal funding for our issue will remain flat
- City will continue to have an affordable housing shortage

Step 2: Determine which conditions you are unsure of. For example:

- Society will get more collaborative or more selfish
- The economy will get better or get worse
- Giving will decrease or increase
- Local elected official will match federal government of policy or do the opposite
- Consumers will want more mass-produced goods or more custom-created goods
- More people will get involved in the democratic process or fewer people will get involved

Step 3: Create a diagram that shows four possible scenarios. For example, one axis could be that more people move to cities or more people want to live in suburbs and the other axis could be that the people prefer collaborative transportation or individual transportation.

Step 4: Brainstorm your actions in each of those quadrants. What are the opportunities and challenges in that scenario? For example, if more people want to live in the city and they prefer collaborative transportation, a bus or light-rail would be a good local transportation option. If more people live in the city and they prefer individual transportation, more bicycle lanes would be useful.

One of the four scenarios will come to pass, and you will be prepared with possible solutions. The case study below describes what the Oxford scenarios planning model looks like in action.

Case Study: Scenario Planning for a New Federal Administration

After Trump was elected president, many of the foundations and nonprofits that I worked with become frozen with indecision. They knew that there were significant changes on the horizon but weren't sure what they would be.

To help clarify the future, I started leading groups of philanthropists and nonprofit leaders through scenario-planning exercises to help them think about what this national change in leadership would mean for funding of local human services nonprofits. To do this, we started by picking a handful of national conditions that we were pretty sure would change. Here is that list:

- Changes in immigration laws, especially impacting Muslim and Hispanic communities
- Decreases in civil rights protections
- Increase in protests
- Changes in tax laws and tax decreases for wealthy taxpayers
- Changes to the Affordable Care Act
- Increased investments in small businesses
- Decreases in federal grants for human services organizations

What we didn't know was whether our local government would match the federal landscape or serve as a contrast. We also didn't know if local foundations would increase their endowments payouts to better support local human service needs or if they would keep their funding steady. We developed an image that looked like this:

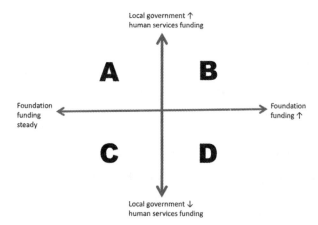

Then we had groups develop a list of opportunities, challenges, and needs in each of the four possible scenarios. We did this with a large visual with the above image and sticky notes in three colors for the opportunities, challenges, and needs. We left the visual up in our conference room for a few weeks so that organizations using the space could add to the scenarios. Through this activity, organizations could prepare for four possible futures.

Here are some examples of the ideas that local nonprofits and foundations came up with for each possible scenario.

Scenario A: Increased local government funding, foundation funding stays steady

Opportunities:
- more collaboration between foundations and local government
- foundations may tie an advocacy strategy to existing funding
- more training and support for applications to local government grant programs

Challenges:
- ensuring that marginalized communities can access local government programs
- weaker incentives for charitable giving mean that new fundraising strategies will have to be developed
- increased pressure for government regulations of foundations from nonprofits and the general public

Needs:
- public policy work to push for more local funding to cover lost federal funding and to help elected officials understand nonprofits
- increased donation drives and fundraising asks, especially targeting individuals

- foundations to clarify and tighten funding priorities or reprioritize grantmaking areas

Scenario B: Increased local government funding, foundation funding increases

Opportunities:
- highlight local public-private collaboration
- complementary advocacy activities
- highlight immigrant contributions in local community

Challenges:
- helping clients navigate changes in human service infrastructure from national cuts

Needs:
- foundations and local government will need to coordinate to cover national government service gaps
- funders will need to clarify new funding direction
- helping nonprofits secure and manage public contracts (including delayed payment)

Scenario C: Decrease in local government funding for human services, foundation funding stays steady

Opportunities:
- opportunity for large-scale organizing and mobilizing
- impact investing to stretch foundation dollars
- foundations could increase public-policy savvy to advocate for community needs and educate policymakers

Challenges:
- community protests
- foundations may be reluctant to challenge policies that favor the wealthy (nonprofits may do the same to protect fundraising interests)
- eliminating services in a way that will least impact communities in need

Needs:
- support for nonprofits that help citizens decipher fake news from real news
- resources to combat cuts in government funding
- foundations to reduce administrative burdens on already strapped grantees

Scenario D: Decreased local government funding, foundation funding increases

Opportunities:
- increase in volunteerism to meet continued community needs that are no longer met by local and national government
- 501(c)(4) organizations may actively work to change local elected officials
- increased public policy interests from foundations to increase government funding (local and national)

Challenges:
- foundations won't have enough resources to fill gaps of government; this will have to be highlighted to elected officials and media
- identifying marginalized communities that can no longer access government programs

- local government programs may be in competition with non-profits for funding

Needs:
- support for effective nonprofit consolidations or new collaborations to decrease overhead costs
- ability to triage nonprofit clients and reach those with greatest need

A few interesting things happen when you do a scenario activity like this:
- **You move from indecision to action.** Once you have lowered the number of possibilities, it gets easier to imagine the future and what your tactics would look like for each possible outcome.
- **You identify positive opportunities.** No matter how dire a scenario looks, there are always positive opportunities you can create if you develop a strategy beforehand.
- **Some signs of how to move forward emerge.** In even the most confusing circumstances, sometimes a common thread of opportunity will emerge through multiple scenarios. In the Trump election example, we found that across all scenarios there would be an increased interest from foundations in mission-related investments, an increase in community volunteerism to support human services nonprofits, and an increased interest in the public policy process amongst social-sector leaders. We adjusted programming and staff time right away to meet those emerging opportunities.

FutureGood All-Star:

Tawanna Black, CEO and founder of the Center for Economic Inclusion

The Center for Economic Inclusion is a regional cross-sector organization created to disrupt market forces and strengthen civic infrastructure in order to catalyze an inclusive, prosperous economy for all. Its participants—which include employers, trainers, fundraisers, and a growing group of other stakeholders—work together to close the employment and wealth gaps for minorities by improving access to transit systems and training while addressing the growing demand for talent and the quest for opportunity.

Under Tawanna's leadership, the center has crafted a bold vision:

"Let's imagine closing this region's growing racial and economic disparities: employers are able to meet their talent needs with local hires, we enjoy thriving cultural corridors in neighborhoods throughout the region; we attract businesses because of our diversity, not in spite of it; and our transit systems support employers and employees with access to work, shop, and play for everyone.

"Let's imagine working TOGETHER with other regional leaders, sharing your experiences and expertise in peer learning and action networks to support real change, in real time so our collective imagination becomes reality."

Bold visions like this align stakeholders around a positive vision of the future. This ensures that resources and time are focused on making that shared vision come to light.

What is the bold vision for the world you are trying to create?

Go Do It!

Here are some techniques to bring scenario planning to your work:

- **Figure out what has already been done.** Find examples of scenarios that have been created for the issues you care about. For example, google *senior housing scenarios.* You may not agree with all of the scenarios, but they will be good food for thought.

- **Stretch your scenario muscle.** This about how your organization would react if a specific scenario came true. What would an elimination of the food-stamp program mean for your services? How would you react if a light-rail line were put right in front of where you provide program services? What if all local businesses were prioritizing hiring veterans? Thinking about the opportunities and challenges for many types of scenarios makes you more prepared if that scenario comes true.

- **Make scenario planning a part of your regular process.** If you are starting strategic planning, think about how to make scenario planning a tool in your process. Find consultants that have expertise in scenario planning. In my consulting work, I lead nonprofits, foundations, and social-purpose businesses through scenario planning workshops. Kedge, founded by Frank Spencer, also leads fantastic scenario planning activities.

CHAPTER 08:

GO DEVELOP A POSITIVE VISION

"If you want to build a ship, don't drum up people to collect wood and don't assign them tasks and work, but rather teach them to long for the endless immensity of the sea."

—Unknown

There are many examples of individuals coming together to craft a new vision for the future, but one of the most powerful is the creation of the Niagara Movement. In response to lynchings of African Americans—and in contrast to Booker T. Washington's call for African Americans to be more accommodating to the injustices that they were facing after slavery—W.E.B. Du Bois drafted a call for "organized determination and aggressive action on the part of men who believed in Negro freedom and growth."

Out of this call, the Niagara Movement was born. More than fifty men and women gathered on the Canadian side of Niagara Falls to develop a declaration of principles outlining a new future for African Americans. These principles laid out expectations for civil liberty, economic opportunity, education, justice, and the end of segregation.

The conference concluded on Sunday, August 19, 1906, with the reading of "An Address to the Country," written by W.E.B. Du Bois. "We will not be satisfied to take one jot or tittle less than our full manhood rights. We claim for ourselves every single right that belongs to a freeborn American, political, civil and social; and until we get these rights we will never cease to protest and assail the ears of America. The battle we wage is not for ourselves alone but for all true Americans."

The passion and the energy that formed the Niagara meeting happened because the vision was so important and so clear. It wasn't small issues that W.E.B. Du Bois was asking them to take on; it was helping America live up to the promise of the American Dream, that every US citizen should have an equal opportunity to achieve success and prosperity through hard work, determination, and initiative. While the Niagara Movement only lasted a few years, it created the conditions and shared values that led to the development of the NAACP, and it laid the framework for civil rights efforts in many communities.

As we think about how to create a shared, positive vision of the future, we should keep in mind the creation of the Niagara Movement, because the hardest part of creating a vision is agreement on what success looks like. People often say, "If we can take a man to the moon, why can't we end poverty?" The reason it is so much easier to take a man to the moon is that we agree on what success looks like. An astronaut leaves Earth and lands on the moon and then safely returns home. We know the exact location and we know what a successful outcome would look like. When we talk about something like ending poverty, do we mean people that make under $15,000 a year? What about families that can't afford rent in areas like San Francisco but make $50,000 a year? Do we just mean people with families, or do we also mean single people? US citizens only or visa holders? Would someone have to be working to qualify for the solution? What about mothers with children under six months old? What about people who are disabled and unable to work? Because we haven't come to an agreement about what a successful outcome would look like, we can't be successful. As we discussed in the chapter on loving the problem, we often spend too much of our time thinking about what we don't want (poverty), instead of what we do want (any person working forty hours a week, going to school, or caring for a child should be able to comfortably afford housing, food, and healthcare in every city and town in America).

I have a lot of experience convening people to solve difficult societal problems. The hardest step in any of those efforts is creating a shared vision of what success looks like. One way that I've found to do this is to create a fifty-year vision of success. This allows people to really be hopeful and clear about what real success would look like, not just what they think they would be able to accomplish in a shorter timeframe. It also takes ego and fear of new work off of the table. When you are working on shorter timeframes, people are often jockeying for credit or are worried about how much new work will be on their plate if the project moves forward. This stifles creativity and the ability to really stretch and consider new solutions. Looking at fifty years gets people to start to be in the place of legacy. They start to ask themselves questions about what they want the world to look like for their children and grandchildren, and they set a higher bar for success. A magical thing happens when you can get people to be in this place of imagination; suddenly, people find it easier to work through thorny issues, assume good intentions about others that are around the table for the process, and feel better about the agreements that they make about what success looks like. After all of that hard work is done, fifty-year visions start to materialize a lot more quickly because the map of where we are all going to is clear. I have seen fifty-year visions start coming to life in year two or three of projects because everyone was pulling in the same direction.

Here are some steps to craft a vision:

Step 1: Set the Table

The most critical step is deciding who will be at the table and who are the right convening partners. I try to find a core group of three to five people with diverse backgrounds and experiences who I know are passionate about the issue we are working on and have a similar set of values guiding their work. I look for people who share my radical vision of what is possible in the future, who can bring their full selves into the process (not just their job titles), who are patient but have a sense of urgency, and who are generous with their time and their expertise. I first host a small dinner with this group (see 831 dinner model in chapter 6), and at the end of that dinner, I figure out who is committed to doing deeper work together. I then ask that group to use its relationship capital to bring together a larger group of fifteen to twenty people. If I were convening a group around regional development, I might bring together a group like this:

- An economic development expert from a local university
- an organizer who has worked with local residents across multiple neighborhoods
- a small-business owner
- an artist who lives in the region
- a poet or novelist with local roots
- an environmental expert with a background in how access to green space impacts neighborhoods
- a human-centered design expert with a connection to local community

- a regional resident who has expertise on future trends, education, housing, health, community building, business trends, civic engagement, youth issues, senior issues, disabilities, equity, transportation, and other issues of critical local concern.

Notice that I didn't pick people like the mayor, head of a local university, or CEO of a Fortune 500 company. I have found that in these processes people with big titles are often brought in but don't often have the time for or interest in being part of a learning process. You don't want people at the table who will give speeches and expect everyone else to run around and implement their vision. You need to create a more equal playing field, where every single participant has something to learn and share during the process. That doesn't mean that you exclude the bigwigs; just wait to bring them in til it is time to build buy-in and implement the vision.

Step 2: Decide on Your Shared Values

Developing a set of shared values about how you treat each other and how you think about community in this process is a critical step. This can take time and is developed both formally and informally. I suggest that the first meetings in this process take place over meals, preferably over dinner. You are building relationships and community, and that makes it easier to agree on a shared set of values. Values may include any of the following:

- We assume good intentions when we are working together.
- We each lead in our spheres of influence and take turns leading at this table.
- We are developing a vision that will strengthen our community for future generations.
- When we are together, we are fully present. No cellphones or side conversations.

- We are all busy but we make time for this process. We start on time and we all attend most meetings.
- What is said in this room stays in this room, but what is learned in this room is shared with our community. We expect privacy and shared learning.

Find what is right for your particular group, and make sure that those values are documented and referred to often. I list value statements on the meeting agendas of any group that I organize because it becomes a persistent reminder of the values that we share.

Step 3: Craft the Vision
After the table is set and values are agreed upon, it's time to get to work. This group should use a preferred-vision process (see chapter 7) to develop a shared vision. Be as clear as possible about what your community would look like if the problem that you are working on were fully solved. Some examples:

- Amnesty International: *Our vision is a world in which every person enjoys all of the human rights enshrined in the Universal Declaration of Human Rights and other international human rights standards.*
- Conservation International: *We imagine a healthy, prosperous world in which societies are forever committed to caring for and valuing nature, for the long-term benefit of people and all life on Earth.*
- Teach for America: *One day, all children in this nation will have the opportunity to attain an excellent education.*
- Feeding America: *A hunger-free America.*
- Habitat for Humanity: *A world where everyone has a decent place to live.*

Develop a vision together that gets people excited and a little bit scared about how big the vision is. This is what keeps a group motivated in the long term.

Step 4: Test the Vision

Building a prototype of the idea is the best way to test it. Have smalls teams create a visual that shows how a neighborhood would look if they implemented your vision of human-centered design or a school-day schedule that shows how students would be spending their time if homework were done in class and lectures were listened to at home using Khanh Academy. Spend some time together comparing the prototypes to see what they have in common and what is different. Use that knowledge to refine the prototype.

Share those prototypes with your planning group, other interested community members, and people that have never heard about the work that you are doing but have a vested interest in your success.

Step 5: Build the Base

Think about who would have to be brought in for the vision to work, and then who in the existing network has the relationships and influence to get that person engaged.

It's sometimes helpful to do a power-mapping process for more critical targets. In an example where you are trying to get a county commissioner on board for a new regional plan your group has developed, the process would look like this:

Determine your target. Which institution is most closely involved ? Who can move that institution? Who is the key decision maker here?

Example: The county is the most critical stakeholder to move the plan forward and the county commissioner is the most powerful

force in the county. Focus on the chair of the county commission-
ers, Irene Fernando.

Determine key influencers of your target. Who are the people that
can influence the target to embrace your plan? Consider past co-
workers, donors, family, and other personal relationships. Who in
your network is connected?

Example: Irene Fernando was the former co-executive director of Students Today Leaders Forever. She lives in Minneapolis
and works for Thrivent Financial.

Create a visual with Irene in the middle using a mind map tool.
I like to use Canva.com's mind map template. Here is an example:

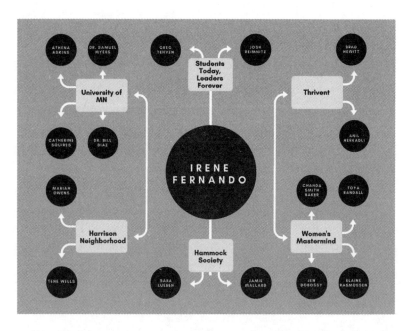

Identify the power players. Sometimes when you do power mapping, you find that there are people who are connected to many of
your targets or have multiple connections to your target. Prioritize

those relationships because they will make your organizing more effective if you can get them on your side.

Reach out to your connection and make the pitch. See if they are willing to meet with the target with you or to present the idea on your behalf.

Step 6: Expand the Vision with Implementors

In his book *Seven Keys to Imagination: Creating the Future by Imagining the Unthinkable and Delivering It,* Piero Morosini develops a critical step for making a vision become a reality. He encourages you to test your prototype with a fresh set of multi-complementers: players "whose products, services, or technologies reduce the costs of building the prototype and increase its attractiveness to people." He says that "multi-complementors have an almost magical effect on the prototype that is being built, making even the most radical and unthinkable ideas of a new future possible." This is where things that once seemed impossible start to come together effortlessly because the vision is matched with the implementors that will make it possible. The clarity of vision and collegiality of the initial group will be attractive to the implementors, who may not have had the patience for the whole process but can add lots of value to a part of the work moving forward.

Brainstorm which types of multi-complementors would be the most useful for your project. The find the best players that work in those spaces locally, nationally, or even internationally to strengthen your plans.

For example, if you were developing a transportation vision for your town, you might want to connect with the nonprofit 8 80 Cities, which has a model of designing cities for people aged eight and aged eighty. Their framework could move your local planning forward with an eye toward accessible design.

Case Study: Experience Trips to Craft a New Vision

I think we sometimes have two conflicting ideas of travel. One is personal travel, the romantic idea of going to an exotic location and exposing yourself to new flavors, sights, and ways of thinking. Travel as a pause button on our often hectic lives, so we can refresh and reenter the fray with a new sense of purpose.

The other is business travel, which for those of us in the social sector means cramped airline seats, quick trips to conferences held in lookalike hotel ballrooms, and plenty of rubber chicken dinners. There are sparks of great ideas, but they are easily extinguished as you try to focus on both the session at hand and the unrelenting emails that drag you back to the office.

When I proposed to my staff that MCF lead an early childhood delegation of funders, practitioners, researchers, and civic leaders to Sweden, I think many of them envisioned the business trip described above on steroids. What we got instead were the sparks of brilliance by enriching our business travel with the relationship-building and wonder more often associated with personal travel.

In September 2015, twenty delegates—including funders, elected officials, professors, representatives from early childhood programs, researchers, and others—traveled with me to Sweden. We spent five days meeting with government officials, NGOs, parents, and children to begin to understand the infrastructure and funding tied to Sweden's world-renowned education system.

We also met university professors dedicated to educating the next generation of early childhood teachers, and we toured three types of preschool programs to better understand the classroom experiences of Swedish children. The visits were thoughtfully curated by our tour guide, and they gave us time to really dig in and ask questions to help us answer our most pressing question: What could this mean for kids in Minnesota?

While the official visits were critical, I think the moments that felt more like personal travel will endure. Walking through Old Town Stockholm to help a fellow delegate find just the right souvenir for her new grandchild while conversing about what outdoor preschool education looks like in Duluth. Standing together on a city bus, being asked politely but loudly to move from the baby carriage section, and realizing that society is very different when children and families are at the center. Sitting in a restaurant built in the 1300s on the grounds of Uppsala Cathedral and watching delegates with very different ideas of what early childhood should look like discover how much they actually have in common.

All of these experiences are what one delegate member, originally from Denmark, called hygge: the warm feeling of connection and hospitality that opens you up to new ways of being with each other. This space of hygge creates the conditions where trust, respect, and mutual joy become the foundation for doing something very different in our local communities.

I believe experiential travel has an important place in our work. We grow by leaving our little corner of the world and exploring what can be learned from a very different corner of the world, and our communities are better off because of it. We get sparks of brilliance enriched with wonder and relationship. I strongly believe that seeing a community that functions in the way that you'd like to see yours operate is a transformative process. It opens your eyes to what is possible and can get a group of stakeholders on the same page.

If you are planning your own experience trip, a few tips:

Carefully curate your delegation. Make sure you have a diverse group that looks at the problem from different angles. For my trips, I try to include a mix of grantmakers, nonprofit leaders, civic leaders, researchers, business representatives, and people impacted by the problem we are trying to fix.

Find an experienced partner on the ground who can help you navigate an unfamiliar city and culture and help you connect with the right local partners to help you understand why they are so successful.

Think of the trip as the middle of the process. Pre-work helps you get on the same page and better understand local context. After the trip, you'll need plenty of time to debrief and plan the next steps.

Away doesn't need to be far. You don't need to necessarily go abroad to see a successful model in action. Sometimes going to a nearby city can have the same impact.

Go Do It!

Here are some ways you can develop a positive vision of the future:

Pick your issue. Decide which issues you are passionate enough about to engage in this process. This work can be long and frustrating, so it needs to be important enough to you that you will continue to move forward even when it gets hard.

Pick your people. Pull together the right group to craft the vision. A Jeffersonian dinner is always a great start because it allows you to test out the group dynamics without making a long-term commitment.

Look beyond your immediate network to get the right people at the table.

Bring a visionary mindset. Bring this mindset to the tables you are part of. This isn't always about creating a new table to develop a plan for the future. You may already be sitting with groups of people that can be doing this type of work but have gotten stuck. Share what you have learned in this chapter with the group's leadership or facilitator and see if that jumpstarts the process.

FutureGood All-Star:

Movement Generation and EDGE Funders Alliance

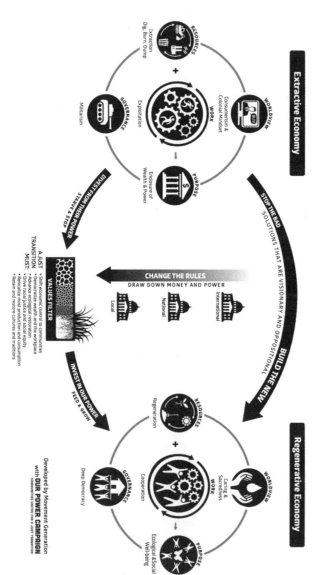

I hosted an experience trip to Barcelona a few years ago and met with some of the team members at Movement Generation and EDGE Funders Alliance. They have been convening a process to help foundations learn how to leverage their grants to transition the economy to a more ecologically sustainable and socially just model. They have developed a beautiful model of the metamorphosis of our economy from "extractive" to "regenerative," which is necessary for us to sustain. We currently live in a "dig, burn, dump" economy, which isn't sustainable and destroys people and the environment in the process. The purpose of this economy is to enhance the wealth of shareholders at all costs. The organizations have imagined a regenerative economy as a replacement. The purpose of this model is the ecological and social well-being of us all. The interesting thing about a metamorphosis is that you take advantage of the old materials as they die to be the power to create the new thing. Systemic change is hard, but if you harness the power of the existing system to create the new system, you benefit from that momentum. For example, forward-thinking car companies aren't asking us to walk everywhere. They are saying, "Try this electric car. It is similar to what you are used to and uses the same road infrastructure, but it has a smaller environmental footprint." The next step of this transition would be to keep using an electric car without owning it, just accessing it through a ride-sharing app or a self-driving car fleet in the not-so-distant future.

Envisioning an entirely new environmental and economic system isn't easy work, but the Movement Generation and EDGE Funders Alliance team took some critical steps (that we have discussed in this chapter) not just to develop this model but also to ensure that the model spread and was used by funders.

- **Set the table.** In this effort, funders and community organizations developed the vision together.

- **Decide on shared values.** There had already been a lot of thought put into what a just transition would look like. This team surveyed the existing initiatives that fell within the just transition parameters to determine what shared values and core principals were underlying that work.
- **Craft the vision.** For this particular visioning process, an easy-to-understand visual was needed to make a complicated process clearer. The team invested in design to make sure that that happened.
- **Test the vision.** This vision was tested with community organizations that were already working on the issue of a just transition with funders who may have known very little about this work. The messaging needed to ring true for both parties.
- **Build the base.** Learning tools were developed for community organizations and for funders to help share this model.
- **Expand with implementors.** By organizing venues for co-learning amongst funders and community organizations, there is a platform for work to be implemented by organizations that have already had an interest in this issue but were not yet aligned with the broader vision.

How might the steps that the EDGE Funders and Movement Generation took to build their model work for your issue?

CHAPTER 9:

GO DEVELOP A FUTURE-FOCUSED ORGANIZATION

"We can't shift everyone,
shift those we can boldly."

—John Kobara

The Stop, Look, Go framework is a useful tool for individuals or projects that are trying to create a new future, but it is most powerful when it is unleashed throughout an organization. Now is a critical time for organizations to understand and create what is next, because nonprofits are losing their monopoly as the most effective agents of social change. Unless they innovate and evolve, social-purpose businesses, corporations, and social enterprises that are also working on the most critical issues of our day with better tools and a clearer focus will eclipse nonprofits as the most critical change agent.

Foundations aren't immune to this disruption either. Because most foundations are structured to last into perpetuity, we don't worry that disruption will cause a foundation to close in the same way that disruption would cause a nonprofit to close. The real question for foundations that face disruption is whether they are still relevant for the issues and communities that they were designed to serve. That relevancy is being challenged by deep-pocketed individual donors, including celebrities who can bring visibility and support through their platform, crowdfunding campaigns, and social investors.

Disruption changes how we think, behave, do business, learn, and do our day-to-day work. Harvard Business School professor Clayton Christensen describes a disruption as something that "displaces an existing market, industry, or technology and produces something new and more efficient and worthwhile." Netflix disrupted Blockbuster. Uber disrupted the taxi business and may soon disrupt the idea of car ownership. The classroom fundraising platform Donor's Choose is disrupting the school bake sale. The Gates Foundation is disrupting traditional vaccine delivery. Disruption is both a destructive and creative force. Disruption can come from a variety of sources, but the most common are advancement of technology, globalization, changing funding priorities, and changing models of providing service.

Twenty years ago, nonprofit and social enterprise disruption was a rare occurrence. Now, it's a reality that organizations face on a regular basis. My concern is that we are not yet regularly talking about disruption around board tables or with our management teams. I think this is a grave mistake. We are entering a time when many long-standing organizations, some fifty to a hundred years old, have been disrupted and are being Kodak-ed right out of existence.

Here are some ways your organization can both build the resiliency to withstand disruption and to find ways to disrupt yourself to create new innovation:

Make the future a part of your organization's present. A critical step to creating a future-looking organization is to give staff the time to step away from their day-to-day work to envision something new.

3M has a unique future-looking corporate culture that has been replicated by many successful companies. The company owes much of its innovative culture to William McKnight, who was the general manager of the company. In 1948, he told his managers, "Encourage experimental doodling. If you put fences around people, you get sheep. Give people the room they need." Still in place today, the rule lets 3M employees spend up to 15 percent of their work time pursuing projects of their own choice, free to look for unexpected, unscripted opportunities for breakthrough innovations that have the potential to expand the pie. The 15 percent time has been used to create the Post-it note, the first electronic stethoscope with Bluetooth technology, and Cubitron II, a specialized sandpaper that retains each particle's sharp, pyramid shape and that still stumps copycats, despite having been on the market since 2009.

The staff at the 3M Foundation used their 15 percent time to develop an initiative called 3M Impact. This global skills-based service program allows 3M teams to work with social enterprises, nonprofits, and universities in markets all over the world. There, they spend two immersive weeks collaborating with a local nonprofit organization, social enterprise, or government agency to contribute to a solution for a pressing social or environmental issue. Over the course of eight additional weeks, teams use their 15 percent time to continue to develop innovations for the client organizations.

Projects are designed to make a positive economic or social impact on the local organization and community while providing an opportunity for participants to strengthen leadership skills, develop market insights, and spur innovative thinking. 3Mers are encouraged to apply and are selected based on the skill sets needed to support community partners in accomplishing their project goals.

Find future champions. A critical step is to understand who your allies are when it comes to building the future. The Institute for the Future developed a great activity that allows you to visually see who in your organization can be a champion for future-focused work, and you can use it as an organizational icebreaker activity.

Step 1: Ask participants to stand. Explain to them that they will place themselves along a continuum according to their responses in a series of prompts.

Step 2: Provide a practice prompt. For example, ask them to place themselves on the continuum of morning person to night person or introvert to extrovert. Give them thirty seconds to arrange themselves, and then ask different people on different parts of the scale to explain why they choose that spot.

Step 3: Use a series of future-focused prompts repeating this same process:

- I tend to be fearful/excited about the future.
- In my current position I feel empowered/disempowered about helping my organization move toward a positive future. (Be careful of using this question in a group that includes both supervisors and direct staff of the same organization)
- I think technology is bringing us closer together/pushing us further apart.
- I am a risk-taker/risk averse when it comes to making decisions about my personal future.

Doing this sort of activity with a team that you are trying to help be more future-focused allows you to see who can be champions for the work and who will need more support in the process.

Incentivize future-focus to transform the culture. It is very unlikely that every single member of your organization will be a strategic future-thinker, so you need to create organizational incentives to encourage all of your staff to either create the innovation needed to prevent your organization from being disrupted or implement the innovations that other staff have developed.

At the Minnesota Council on Foundations, we identified a trend that racial economic inequalities were growing in our community. As an organization that is committed to helping build more equitable foundations, we had a responsibility to model more equitable spending practices to change that future trend.

We did some investigation and found that less than 4 percent of our spending was with businesses owned by people of color. To remedy this, I set a new goal that 20 percent of staff spending needed to be with POC-owned vendors. We purchased access to a citywide database of businesses owned by people of color, developed an internal list of new businesses to partner with, and added a review of the staff's spending to their annual review.

As a result of these supports and incentives, in the first year, organizational spending with POC-owned businesses shot from less than 4 percent to 67 percent. In that modeling process, we also encouraged our membership to use these businesses as well by sharing our vendor policy, sharing our list of vendors, and asking caterers and facilitators in particular to leave business cards at our events.

Embrace failure. Organizations require a higher level of risk than they did during the Industrial Age. With the fast pace of technology, an organization could lose its whole market share overnight, so they have had to continually experiment. With that innovation and experimentation, there will be more failure, and we have to embrace that as the new normal. As Truman Capote said, failure is "the condiment that gives success its flavor."

We need to build our organizations so that employees are encouraged to experiment and embrace the failure that comes along with it. When we share our failures, both internally and externally, it dissipates the shame and instead creates a culture where we can learn from each other's failures.

Special advice for non-CEO's that want to move their organization to the future:

It is important to recognize that the move to becoming a more future-focused organization does not need to come from an organization's CEO or board. A future-focused vision can come from anywhere in an organization, and direct line staff are more likely to deeply understand the levers that are influencing their area of work.

A great example of this is Robyn Schein at the Minneapolis Foundation. When Robyn was a young donor services officer at the foundation, she realized that all of the foundation's services were geared toward older donors. She knew that there was a coming generational transfer of wealth, and she wanted to help the Minneapolis Foundation be a natural choice for the next generation of donors.

Robyn brought in Sharna Goldseker, a leading expert of next-generation philanthropy, to meet with her management team to help make the case that developing services for the next generation of donors was a good use of organizational time and resources. At the same time, Community Capital Alliance, a volunteer-led nonprofit organization that was developing young professionals through community philanthropy, was looking for a new organizational home. Robyn harnessed both of these opportunities and rebranded the Community Capital Alliance as the Fourth Generation Fund at the Minneapolis Foundation.

Fourth Generation is a hands-on philanthropy experience for young professionals. Members work together to learn about a critical community issue and identify promising efforts to address it. They pool their donations together to make a bigger impact than they could alone. Since 2010 more than one hundred Fourth Generation members have donated, raised, and given away more than $300,000 to address critical issues such as mental health, youth homelessness, food justice, small business development, resources for immigrant populations, aging, and criminal justice reform.

These donors are now better connected to this community foundation that is over a hundred years old, and they are a pipeline for future donations.

If you are not the CEO of your organization but you'd like to implement a new innovation, here are some steps that you can take:

- **Find your allies** inside and outside of the organization. Is there someone else better positioned within the organization to move the idea forward? As Harry Truman said, "It is amazing what you can accomplish if you do not care who gets the credit."
- **Make the case.** Find the internal and external data that clarifies the trend that you are noticing.
- **Find your collaborators.** Often an external collaborator, in your sector or outside of it, can help move work forward more quickly. Figure out who is on a similar path. When asked recently about how the nonprofit model needs to change, my BFF Sir Richard Branson made the case for cross-sector collaboration by saying, "More collaborative efforts. We need the collective efforts of countries and companies to step up and play their part—setting strong goals, having clear plans, and openly demonstrating progress."

- **Market, market, market.** Lots of great ideas have failed to gain traction because they weren't marketed. Make sure that you can clearly and succinctly describe your idea. Would a catchy name or an informative one-pager help? Then invest the time in marketing to make sure that your idea gets a fighting chance.

Case Study: How Strong Values Can Prepare Organizations for an Uncertain Future

For much of its history, Ben & Jerry's ice cream has been a leader in social enterprise. From their commitment to ethically sourcing their ingredients, industry-leading practices of paying their entry-level employees a living wage, and commitment to community through a robust philanthropic strategy, they have been a leader in the corporate social responsibility space. In 1999, that history could have quickly came to an end.

Ben & Jerry's was courted by two companies (Dreyer's and Unilever), and as a public company, they had a duty to their shareholders to consider those offers. The board rejected the offer from Dreyer's, but Ben & Jerry's board chairman Jeff Furman said, "The whole board eventually came to the understanding that they could negotiate with Unilever, not just for a better financial offer but also for their company values to remain after the sale." In that process, the board negotiated for nine of the eleven board seats of Ben & Jerry's into perpetuity, a formula for ongoing donations to the Ben & Jerry's Foundation tied to sales growth, the ability to set employee wages, and full control over product ingredients and marketing.

When the deal was announced in 2000, the press release said, "Shareholders will be rewarded, Ben & Jerry's employees will be protected; the current social mission of Ben & Jerry's will be encouraged and well-funded, which will lead to improved performance in this area, and an opportunity has been offered for Ben & Jerry's to contribute to Unilever's social practices worldwide."

Both companies said that Ben & Jerry's would continue as it always had and that Unilever would initially commit 7.5 percent of Ben & Jerry's profits to a foundation . That percentage has increased over time, utilizing a formula tied to sales growth. Unilever also agreed not to reduce jobs or alter the way the ice cream is made. Unilever would also contribute $5 million to the foundation, create a $5 million fund to help minority-owned businesses and others in poor neighborhoods, and distribute $5 million to employees in six months.

As a result of this sale, Ben & Jerry's is having an even larger social impact than they did as an independent company. Their sales have increased since the sale, and as a result their foundation's giving and number of employees paid a living wage are increasing as well. Unilever recognized the unique value that Ben & Jerry's brings to their portfolio of brands and has been thinking about how to expand that thinking to their other brands.

Having a social mission is a competitive advantage, but it only works if those values are core to your organization and shared by your leadership and employees. The board of Ben & Jerry's makes sure that those values remain.

Go Do It!

Here are some ways you can develop a future-focused organization:

- **Make time for the future.** Makes sure employees are able to set aside time to think about the future and make it an expected part of the organizational culture.
- **Build trust.** Change moves forward more quickly when there are a shared vision and a sense of trust. Make sure that

your organization is constantly building trust internally and externally.

- **Identify your allies.** Identifying your future champions throughout the organizational hierarchy will ensure that you don't just have leadership buy-in; the staff that will be implementing changes will also be strategic allies.
- **Fail fast.** Allowing employees to take risks and accept a level of failure is necessary to succeed.
- **Measure progress.** Keeping track of key indicators and helping the team see progress is critical to keeping up momentum and motivation.

FutureGood All-Stars:

Alicia Garza, Opal Tometi, and Patrisse Cullors, cofounders of Black Lives Matter

Born online in 2013 following George Zimmerman's acquittal for killing seventeen-year-old Trayvon Martin and translated to the streets after the killing of Michael Brown in Ferguson, #BlackLivesMatter is an organization, a decentralized peace movement, and a rallying cry for racial justice. The organization seeks to reaffirm the humanity of African Americans and to remind the world that when police officers and domestic terrorists kill Black people, they must be held accountable.

The work has innovated as the Black Lives Matter Network joined more than fifty other African American civil rights groups to create the Movement for Black Lives. The Movement for Black Lives engaged in a yearlong process of convening local and national groups and receiving feedback from the broader African American community through surveys, national calls, and research to develop a united agenda and shared political platform.

The organization's platform, "A Vision for Black Lives: Policy Demands for Black Power, Freedom and Justice," has six demands:

1. End the war on Black people
2. Reparations
3. Invest-Divest
4. Economic justice
5. Community control
6. Political power

Each demand outlines the demands, the problem, the solution, and actions to be taken at local, state, and federal levels.

Black Lives Matter has evolved from a hashtag to a political movement by constantly innovating to meet new demands on the organization and new opportunities for collaboration and partnership.

How can you build visibility for the cause that you care about?

CHAPTER 10:

GO BE A PART OF THE FUTUREGOOD MOVEMENT

*"We did not come to fear the future.
We came here to shape it."*

—Barack Obama

We are living through a time of massive societal transformation, but this isn't the first time in modern history that we have undergone a transformation so significant.

During the Industrial Revolution, which started in 1760, society went through extraordinary changes that impacted the sort of work people did, how cities were built, the scope of our economy, how governments operated, and how families interacted. As a society, we moved from an eighty-hour work week that depended on child labor and slave-like conditions for factory workers to the forty-hour work week with protections for workers that considered their safety.

During this time of great transition, the Lunar Society of Birmingham was born in England. The group shared a fascination with the emerging science of the time, unusual ideas, and their application to society. The name of the society was derived from their habit of meeting on the Sunday nearest the full moon to share ideas, food, and drinks. Members included:

- Matthew Boulton, builder of an advanced steam engine
- James Watt, an engineer
- Erasmus Darwin, a philosopher, doctor, inventor, poet, and grandfather of Charles Darwin
- Joseph Priestley, the radical preacher and chemist who first isolated oxygen
- William Small, who taught natural philosophy and mathematics to Thomas Jefferson
- John Whitehurst, an instrument and clock maker

The group was even connected to Benjamin Franklin through their common interest in electricity. Robert Schofield, who wrote about the society in his 1963 book, *The Lunar Society of Birmingham*, which described them as "a brilliant microcosm of that scattered community of provincial manufacturers, and professional men who found England a rural society with an agricultural economy and left it urban and industrial."

I'm not telling you about an obscure 1760s men's social club and philosophical society just because I think it is an interesting historical tidbit; I'm telling you because I think we need to bring back this idea for the technological revolution that we are going through now.

I think we need to build a FutureGood society that is designed to help us debate and frame the future of our industries and our communities. We need to look at the technological advances of today, share novel ideas, and think about their application to our rapidly changing society.

We need to build our attention span for big ideas and reward thinkers, businesses, and nonprofits that are building long-term visions for the issues that we care about. What our society desperately needs now is leaders from all sectors, backgrounds, and walks of life thinking about and shaping the future.

I believe that *you* are one of those leaders.

Here are some steps to be a FutureGood movement builder:

Read this book with others. The challenges facing society are so important that we need more than just a handful of people who are thinking about the future; we need a movement. If every person who read this book were to organize ten people to read it together, a powerful exponential shift would be possible in how we see our communities and create what comes next.

Book clubs are a surprisingly useful tool for social change. In an era where we are hungry for connection and shared meaning, book clubs connect people around a common idea and allow the participants to go on that journey together. As you are working to build your future-focused mindset, having allies who are also on the journey with you is really helpful for your personal growth.

Sign your group up at www.TristaHarris.org/bookclub to get special facilitation resources to help your FutureGood book club envision a new future together.

Host an 831 dinner on the future of your issue area. In chapter 6, we talked about dinners as a way to build community and develop new ideas. Commit to hosting an 831 dinner about a topic that you are passionate. Invite a diverse group with differing backgrounds and experiences to expand your thinking and your network. Use this as a launching pad to envision a new future.

Join an existing network. Is there a local futurism meet-up that you could join? Is there a study trip to see the future of the issue you care about in action?

Join the FutureGood Society. If you are ready to bring your future vision skills to the next level, I'd like to invite you to apply for membership to the FutureGood Society—a carefully curated community of visionaries committed to building a better future. Through exclusive access to the world's foremost experts, international site visits to see the future in action, and coaching with me, members build their capacity to use the tools of futurism to solve social problems.

As our country moves toward a time of more uncertainty, keeping an eye toward the future allows us to imagine beyond the confusion of today and instead build a new tomorrow. Members include CEOs, philanthropists, social entrepreneurs, nonprofit visionaries, and civic leaders.

Members are selected through an application process, as the group is kept purposefully small. Membership gives you access to monthly webinars, an international learning tour, special events, and a curated community of people planning with imagination and wisdom for a better future.

Case Study: The Original FutureGood Masterminders, Jennifer DoBossy, Irene Fernando, Toya Randall, Elaine Rasmussen, and Chanda Smith-Baker

In 2017, I was in my second year of a Bush Fellowship. Anita Patel, who is the Bush Foundation Leadership programs director, describes the fellowship in this way: "Bush Fellows are exceptional leaders who have made the most of the opportunities in their lives. We believe the well-being of our region is directly impacted by investing in individuals who will shape the future."

I had three goals during my fellowship:

1. Enhance my futurism skills with additional professional education
2. Learn how to make the tools of futurism more accessible for people who are making the world a better place
3. Don't die at my desk

The third goal came from seeing many Black women sacrifice their health and well-being as they worked to strengthen community. I wanted to learn how to do good work in a way that was sustainable. After the first year of the fellowship, Anita told me that I was doing great on the first two goals but she wasn't seeing any tangible actions that I was taking to not die at my desk. It was a good reminder that I needed to be proactive with my self-care goals. As I tried to find a retreat, I became more and more disillusioned. Some programs were more immersive, but going to the woods to sleep in bunk beds and talk about resilient leadership for twelve hours a day sounded miserable. I also wasn't interested in being a part of a leadership cohort program where we met monthly in a bleak conference room and I was one of the only people of color. In those spaces, real self-care often feels like an afterthought. I wanted to be in a space where we were actually rejuvenating, while we talked about how to make these practices a part of our ongoing habits.

With the encouragement of Irene Fernando, a fellow in my Bush Cohort, I created the FutureGood Mastermind Retreat. Masterminds are a concept developed by Napoleon Hill in his 1937 book *Think and Grow Rich*. He describes it as:

"Coordination of knowledge and effort, in a spirit of harmony, between two or more people, for the attainment of a definite purpose. . . . The process of mind blending here described as a 'Master Mind' may be likened to the act of one who connects many electric batteries to a single transmission wire, thereby 'stepping up' the power passing over that line by the amount of energy the batteries carry. . . . Each mind, through the principle of mind chemistry, stimulates all the other minds in the group."

The FutureGood Mastermind was built around the idea that we could each create our own unique dent in the world by providing each other with support, accountability, and a space for us to retreat and refresh ourselves. For our first retreat, I rented a beautiful mansion near the ocean in Pacific Grove, California, and five women and I spent five days setting powerful goals and helping each other develop strategies to accomplish those goals.

In the first year after the retreat, each FutureGood masterminder had significant professional and personal growth. Members started businesses, switched sectors, built an organization, ran for public office, and built their platforms for greater impact.

Each of the original five masterminders has committed to growing this network of women and to being a source of encouragement and support for new participants. Since that initial retreat, more than one hundred women are now a part of the FutureGood Network, and the power of women taking time for themselves and their goals is continuing to grow. If you want to learn more about upcoming FutureGood Masterminds, Google search "Trista Harris" and "Mastermind."

Go Do It!

Here are a few ways to build a FutureGood Movement:
- **Make the future a topic of conversation**. Write op-eds about the future in your local paper. Send reporters thank-you notes when they cover stories about the long-term future. Host events where the future is the topic of conversation.

- **Help our elected officials develop a long-term mindset.** Vote for future-focused candidates and proposals. Ask questions about the long-term future at candidate forums to figure out where your potential elected officials stand on issues like climate change, artificial intelligence, and self-driving cars. Educate elected officials about the future of the issue you care about, and help them see unintended consequences of short-term policy decisions.

- **Think about your personal impact on the future.** What sort of businesses are you supporting with your spending? Based on their corporate values and practices, are they creating the sort of future you would like to see? Where do you invest your money? If it is independently or through your organization's investment plan, do some investigations into how your resources are being used. Are those investments building the type of future you are interested in seeing? Are your charitable donations supporting the type of future that you care about?

- **Bring others along.** How are you building the tribe that cares about the future of your issue? This could include people you work with, people in competing organizations, donors, or that cool speaker you met at the conference. Continuously bring this group together with 831 dinners, create an email newsletter, host a conference, or just connect over happy hour. Agree that you will each do your part to influence the influencers and make your ideal future possible.

FutureGood All-Star:

YOU!

You have all of the tools that you need to build a better future for our communities. You have the drive, the determination, and the knowledge necessary to make tomorrow better than today.

Now all you have to do is take the next step. Take some time to envision the future that you are willing to fight for. The future that you are willing to dedicate your life's work to.

Find the people who will be along with you for that journey. Nurture those relationships and create the space where their ideas and experiences will only make the future you have envisioned brighter.

Once that vision is clear, do the work every single day to make that vision a reality. Do the work in your personal life to make sure that your choices are making that future more likely. Choose a career path that will put you in the best position to make that future happen.

I can't wait to see the future that we are creating together.

CONTACT TRISTA

To get the latest updates and resources to help you build a better future, visit:
www.TristaHarris.org

Trista speaks frequently on helping audiences to build a better future. She can deliver a keynote, half-day, or full-day version of this content, depending on your needs. If you are interested in learning more, please visit her speaking page at:

https://trista-harris.squarespace.com/speak

You can also connect with Trista here:

Blog: www.TristaHarris.org
Twitter: twitter.com/TristaHarris

ARE YOU READY TO UPGRADE YOUR LEADERSHIP?

JOIN A FUTUREGOOD MASTERMIND RETREAT!

Future Good Mastermind Retreats take place in beautiful locations throughout the world, with a carefully curated network of support.

- Develop your ability to predict and shape the future of the issues and communities you care deeply about.
- Expand your network to include visionaries who are making an impact in their communities.
- Give yourself the time and space to consider how to increase your impact in a way that is sustainable in the long-term.

Learn more at
http://trista-harris.squarespace.com/mastermind-retreats

ARE YOU READY TO JOIN THE FUTUREGOOD COMMUNITY?

FutureGood is a community of visionaries committed to building a better future. Through exclusive access to the world's foremost experts, international site visits to see the future in action, and coaching with Trista Harris, Philanthropic Futurist, members build their capacity to use the tools of futurism to solve social problems.

As our country moves toward a time of more uncertainty, keeping an eye toward the future allows us to imagine beyond the confusion of today and instead build a new tomorrow. Members include CEOs, philanthropists, social entrepreneurs, nonprofit visionaries, and civic leaders.

Members receive:
- Access to monthly webinars to increase their futurism skills.
- An international learning tour to see the future in action.
- Special events and first access to other FutureGood events.
- Engagement in a curated community of people planning with imagination and wisdom for a better future.

Learn more at
http://trista-harris.squarespace.com/futuregood-community/

FutureGood
with Trista Harris